SWITCH

A NOVEL

Heather Glenn Vines

Switch: A Novel

Published by:

Aviva Publishing
Lake Placid, NY
(518) 523-1320
www.AvivaPubs.com

Address all inquiries to:
Heather Glenn Vines
heather@vineslines.com
VinesLines.com

ISBN: 978-1-950241-16-3
Library of Congress Control Number: 2022905869

Editor: Tyler Tichelaar, Superior Book Productions
Cover Design and Interior Layout: Fusion Works

Every attempt has been made to properly source all quotes.

Printed in the United States of America
First Edition

2 4 6 8 10 12

To my parents

Grizel and Sterling

For showing me that the impossible isn't.

Acknowledgments

A heartfelt thank you to Greg for offering to wade through my early manuscript and provide invaluable feedback. To Peter for volunteering to do the same and then going one step further by recruiting Jennie. A special thank you to Jennie, to Terry, and to Percy for their insights, edits, and encouraging words. And to my editor, Tyler Tichelaar, for his expertise on all levels of the editing process, as well as his subtle humor and warmth.

Chapter One

Monday morning, 8 a.m.

Maggie hadn't really thought about what she was doing; she was just doing. Moving. And right now, that seemed to be what mattered most. Moving in some direction. What that direction was, well, she'd figure that out later—hopefully. Right now, as the train pulled out of the station, she breathed deeply, letting out what felt like two weeks' worth of stale air.

Phoebe was sound asleep beside her, snoring softly, with her little head bobbing up and down, in rhythm with the train's rocking motion. Maggie reached her hand over and softly stroked her daughter's curly blond hair. Her fingers unconsciously worked to smooth out the tiny tangles that had formed at the bottom of the strands. *A little conditioner*, Maggie thought, *or even a brush. Things will be different now*, she promised herself.

"Tickets. Tickets, please!" the conductor bellowed as he made his way through the car, rocking and swaying his way down the aisle. By the time he reached Maggie's seat, Maggie was convinced he'd been walking on trains for so long that he probably had a difficult time walking on land.

She handed him her two tickets and smiled. "Thank you," she said, and he nodded. It had been at least twenty years since she'd been on a train—not since she was a little girl, traveling across the country with her father. That trip had also been in March, at the tail end of winter, with the promise of spring and just a hint of newness in the air. Her favorite part, as she recalled, was the dining car. She remembered when she was a young child how difficult it had been to get there without falling. But once there, it was a world unlike any other she'd known. Linen table clothes, a waiter dressed like a penguin, and people from all over the country coming together to this one moving car to dine. She and her father had once shared a table with a gentleman from Nebraska. And another time, a family from Florida. Her father loved nothing better than striking up a conversation with a complete stranger, something she'd never been comfortable doing.

Oddly, though, Maggie felt safer now than she had in years, on this train, traveling sixty miles an hour, to nowhere in particular, with Phoebe sleeping peacefully by her side.

Chapter Two

Monday morning, 8 a.m.

"Hey, buddy, you know how long 'til we arrive at the next stop?" Jack asked as he leaned over the seat in front of him. The guy in the pin-striped, gray suit hardly lifted his face, he was so engrossed in his laptop. He simply shrugged Jack off with a slight wave of his hand.

Not the friendliest person, thought Jack as he settled back into his seat and faced forward again. *He didn't have to be a jerk about it, though.* The man's reaction didn't really surprise Jack; in fact, he was becoming more and more aware of such responses, as if he didn't matter or hardly existed. To be honest, he wasn't really looking for an answer. He just wanted someone to talk to, a distraction from his own thoughts. He was returning home, coming back to clean up his mess. No easy task, he considered. Unsettling, at best. Just a few months ago, he had felt differently—so confident and strong. Now he seemed anything but. Going home was just part of his new path. Necessary but terrifying.

Jack stared out the window again, this time noticing the ground was carpeted with a soft dusting of white snow. *Warm, peaceful, inviting*, he thought as he wrapped his coat a little tighter around his shoulders and closed his eyes.

How long had he slept? Jack couldn't say. Based on the early morning light, he guessed it must be around eight o'clock. And guessing was as good as it got with Jack. Because, unlike 98 percent of the population, he didn't have a cell phone. And unlike the other 2 percent, he didn't even have a watch. Up until now, he hadn't really needed one. He rubbed his eyes slowly. When he opened them, Jack found himself being stared at by a little girl with curly blond hair and crisp blue eyes. She was just standing there, watching him—fascinated. Initially, he wasn't sure where he was. Or what was happening. And this young child? Where had she come from? He sat up quickly and wiped the drool off the side of his mouth. She tilted her head to the side, as if to change her view slightly.

"Hello?" he asked with hesitation. She said nothing.

He blinked.

She smiled.

He blinked twice.

She giggled.

Suddenly, the woman one row back on the opposite side of the train jumped up, grabbed the little girl by the arm, and returned her to her seat.

Chapter Three

Monday morning, 8:15 a.m.

"Phoebe, sit. You can't go wandering off. You need to stay right here with me," Maggie scolded. Phoebe lowered her head and stuck out her lower lip a tad. She never liked to be reprimanded. Maybe that was why she seldom if ever crossed the line.

"Let's get out your coloring book and work on that a little," said Maggie, softening a bit. In their hasty departure, Maggie had managed to grab a few essentials—the coats on their backs, a change of clothes for Phoebe, two of her favorite bedtime stories, and her coloring book with crayons. Maggie watched as Phoebe carefully stayed in the lines. Her daughter thoughtlessly twirled her hair with her left hand, and colored with her right.

"Mommy," Phoebe asked as she filled in the outline of a tree with small green strokes, "why didn't Daddy come with us?"

Maggie quietly considered her response. She had known this question would come. She'd been hoping she'd have a little more time before it crossed Phoebe's lips.

"Is your name Maggie?" he had asked softly. It had been eight years earlier. Maggie was much younger. Less worldly. It was a time when she thought of herself as feisty and invincible.

"Yes. It is Maggie. And your name?" she asked even though she already knew the answer. *Matt*, she said quietly to herself.

"Matt. Matt McCauley," he replied as he offered his hand. They shook hands a bit too softly for Maggie's liking. His hand lingered. Hers, on the other hand, was more forceful than it needed to be. She was new to this world of handshaking. It seemed so manly. So definitive. She liked it. The very act of extending her hand out made her feel like she was part of this world to which she didn't belong. This handshake, however, seemed oddly out of sync. *Awkward*, she thought. She would have to work on this some more.

"Are you from the area?" he asked. He smiled in such a way as to suggest he knew damn well she wasn't.

"Yes," she lied.

"Then maybe you can show me around," he whispered as he lowered his six-foot, three-inch frame down to her level. They were standing in line at the cafeteria. She'd just assumed he was from here. She'd heard his name a few times before at the office. He worked in accounting, one office over from hers.

"Well, sure," she said, adding, "I could do that."

"Tomorrow after work?" he asked. "You could be my tour guide. And for your time and effort, I would treat you to dinner, of course. Is there a good Italian place in town? I could really use a pepperoni calzone!" She had nothing going on tomorrow. Or for the rest of the week for that matter. And for once in her life, she wasn't prepared with a quick reason to say no.

"Great! Tomorrow night it is then," he said. He reached out to shake her hand again, as if closing a business deal.

What? Maggie thought, a little puzzled by what had just happened. She'd been caught off guard. She wasn't really looking to connect. Not just yet anyway. She wanted to get settled first. To figure things out a bit. Oh well. She needed to get to know people anyway. She was already isolating too much.

Maggie finished her day at work and headed home. It was a short ten-minute drive through neighborhoods with houses that had been home to three generations, shaded by towering elms. Front porches lined the streets, and tricycles littered the sidewalks. She drove slowly. There was no hurry now. The evening was all hers. Once home, she settled into her routine: dining at the kitchen counter, yesterday's left-over chicken from the deli, this morning's unread newspaper. It wasn't the most exciting life, but it seemed to suit Maggie at the moment.

As she sipped on a slightly warm cup of coffee, Maggie slowly rubbed her temples and thought of her father. "Every object will remain at rest or in uniform motion," he would start. And she would finish "unless compelled to change." "Precisely!" he would exclaim excitedly as if the two of them had just now discovered this theory all by themselves, once again.

Oh, how she wished she could pick up the phone and call her father. She missed his world. The lack of ambiguity. The straight-forward simplicity. Even the beautifully clean, irrefutable laws of physics. But he was gone and had been for two years now. A heart attack. That's what the doctor had said. But Maggie knew. Nothing had attacked his heart. It simply broke.

"Motion," she said out loud as she stood up to clean the morn-ing dishes. "Motion. In spite of me. You would've been proud of me today, Dad."

The next morning, Maggie spent an extra ten minutes get-ting ready for the day. Her favorite sweater. Best pair of jeans. And a touch of blush she found tucked in the back of her drawer. She now knew where to get the best—and only—calzones in Whitefish. Just a few blocks from the office actually. Yet she hadn't found out any-thing more about Matt. *Tonight should be interesting*, she thought. It had been months since she'd been on a date. Okay, maybe years. And she hadn't made the effort to become friends with anyone here in Whitefish. Only acquaintances, she considered as she slid into her car, turned on the engine, and headed left to the office.

Maggie's world was structured with predictable routines. She liked it that way. She had the same breakfast every morning. One cup of black coffee, two pieces of dry whole wheat toast. Took the same route to work. Stopped by the mailroom on the way to her desk. And started each new workday with a blank Post-it note, where she jotted down five things she had to accomplish before she could call it a day. *Routines aren't boring*, she reasoned. *They're efficient. Less time wasted with minor decisions.* As she reached for her Post-it notepad on this particular day, she noticed it wasn't blank at all, which rattled her a bit.

"DINNER WITH MATT. Looking forward to calzones tonight. Meet me in the lobby at 5:30?—Matt."

Maggie looked suspiciously around but saw nothing unusual. Just Rachel at her computer, clicking away mindlessly. When she noticed Maggie staring at her, Rachel stopped typing for a moment, looked up, and said, "Matt from accounting stopped by earlier. I hadn't realized you two knew each other."

"Just met," replied Maggie. "What do you know about him?"

"Not too much. He's kind of cute. I hear he was from this area but moved away years ago. Got married. But something happened there. Not sure what. Something happened to his wife, I think. He's been back for a while now."

Maggie and Rachel had a pile of stuff to work through, so the day went fast. Before Maggie knew it, it was 5:20. She quickly cleaned up her desk and headed downstairs to the lobby.

"Well, hello there," Matt greeted her with a big, warm smile. "Have you figured out where you're taking me?" His smile seemed to grow. It was an odd mixture of warmth, a touch of sarcasm, a hint of playfulness, and a trace of something unsettling. Maggie was intrigued.

"I have, in fact," said Maggie, "discovered where the finest calzones are in all of Whitefish. And fortunately, they are within walking distance from where we are standing right now!" she exclaimed with mocked excitement.

"Perfect," he said. "I'm starving!"

Within minutes, they were entering a cute little Italian pizzeria. Maggie had found it online, but she hadn't actually taken the time to try it in person. They stood at the counter and ordered. The place was somewhat busy, but they spotted a table in the back, which they both instinctively moved toward.

"So, what don't I know about Maggie Larkin?" Matt asked as he bit into his pepperoni calzone.

"What *do* you know?" she replied.

He rattled off a fairly extensive list of facts. "Born in Kalispell. An only child. Mother died when you were eight. Moved out East. Graduated from the University of Virginia. Returned just a few months ago."

"I'm impressed," she said. And she was. "I think that covers everything."

"It couldn't possibly," he flattered her. He had this way of looking at her that made her feel like he was really seeing her. Like she couldn't hide from him. Which made her feel uncomfortable. Exposed. Even vulnerable.

"And I know nothing about you," she said. "You said you weren't from here, yet you grew up here?"

He paused for a moment and then rubbed his left palm with his right hand, back and forth a few times. "Yes, a long time ago," he said. She noticed just a tinge of irritation as he answered her question. "But that was a long time ago," he repeated. "You are by far more interesting. What did you think of Virginia? And how long were you there?" he asked, redirecting their conversation before taking another bite of his calzone.

Back to me, thought Maggie. She wasn't used to talking about herself. And she certainly wasn't used to all of this attention. But she rather liked it.

"Oh, I went for school. Then stayed after that." She thought for a moment. *I was there because that's where Dad was at that particular time.* After her mom died when she was eight, she and her dad had moved a lot: one side of the country to the other, and then back again. Maggie always thought in some way it was as if he were looking for what was no longer there.

"And you've been here in Montana for about three months?" Matt asked.

"Yes," she replied.

"What do you think of Whitefish? People generally love it or not," he said with a whimsical expression.

"It's perfect. It's just what I need right now," she said. Which was true. She loved how small town it felt. And that the people here were friendly without being nosy. There seemed to be enough to do if she were interested. But not so much that it struck her as overwhelming either.

As they finished their calzones and made their way out onto the street, Matt suggested they wander around downtown a bit. "It's a great night for it. Not too cold and the sky's as clear as they come," he said.

They walked along the trail beside the river. The streetlamps softly illuminated their path, making it seem at once eerie and familiar. It wasn't long before Matt had linked his arm through hers and seemed to be guiding her along. Ordinarily, this would've put Maggie a bit on edge, but she found herself comforted by it. The longer they walked like this, the more Maggie opened up to Matt, telling him all kinds of things she'd never shared with anyone else. As Maggie recalled, the entire evening seemed magically surreal.

Years later, when Phoebe asked where she came from, Maggie always thought back to that night. It wasn't the night Phoebe was conceived. But it was the moment Maggie's life changed direction and the space for Phoebe was created.

Chapter Four

Monday morning, 9 a.m.

"Mommy, I'm hungry," Jack heard a little voice say from one seat back and over. *It must be Phoebe, that cute little girl with the blond curls*, he thought. He kind of wished the mom had let her visit with him a bit longer. He loved kids and had always been considered good with them when he was younger. He hadn't had much exposure to them the past four years. But he was pretty sure they hadn't changed much in that time.

"Mom, I want something to eat. Please, Mommy," Phoebe begged.

I'm hungry too, thought Jack. How long had it been since he'd eaten? He wasn't too sure. He was definitely hungry now that he thought about it. *It had to be around eight o'clock in the morning*, figured Jack, as he gazed out on the snow-capped mountains. Because of his tall frame and fast metabolism, he never seemed to get quite enough food to round him out. He had always had that long, lean, hungry look about him.

Bet there's a dining car somewhere on this train, he thought as he stood up and reached in his back pocket for his wallet. He nodded briefly to Phoebe as he walked by, holding on to the back of the seats as he made his way down the aisle, rocking from side to side.

Three cars down, Jack found what he was looking for. To his surprise, only one empty table was left. He sat down quickly and waited for a menu. He noticed other tables seemed to be shared by strangers, one couple introducing themselves to the other. *Interesting*, he thought, *how people in a train's dining car will sit with people they've never met before and do what they typically won't anywhere else—talk to each other.*

As he waited patiently, Jack noticed Phoebe entering the car with her mother.

"Mommy, here's a place for us. Mommy, let's sit here," Phoebe sang out as she pulled her mother along behind her. She plopped down across from Jack and smiled.

"Hello again," he said, smiling as he welcomed Phoebe to his table.

"Do you mind if we sit here?" asked Phoebe's embarrassed mother as she stood politely behind the chair.

"Not at all," said Jack. "There's plenty of room, and besides, I think this young lady and I met earlier. My name is Jack." He reached his hand out to shake Phoebe's. Phoebe giggled a little as she looked to her mom for permission.

Her mom nodded to her, then said, "This is Phoebe. And my name is Maggie," as she sat down beside Phoebe.

Jack found this simple exchange unexpectedly refreshing. Suddenly, he was at a loss for words, which turned out not to be a problem because Phoebe had plenty.

"This is my mom," announced Phoebe proudly. "Do you have a mom?" Then she stopped to consider that maybe he was too old to have a mother.

"I'm actually on my way to see her now," Jack said, which seemed to please Phoebe. "And where are you going, Phoebe?"

A puzzled look came over Phoebe's face as she realized for the first time that she had no idea where she and her mom were headed. After watching this exchange with amusement for a moment, Maggie jumped in. "We're going exploring," she exclaimed nervously, as if the two of them were on a great adventure.

"Yes, exploring!" Phoebe repeated.

Jack studied Maggie for a moment. As a rule, he tended to stay clear of adults. Didn't trust them. But there was something about Maggie, something familiar, unthreatening—yet oddly quirky—that he liked. On the outside, she was pretty in her own way, but not particularly striking. Shoulder-length, straight hair. *Almost the color of Montana earth, a warm brown infused with hints of copper and gold,* he thought as he glanced out the window at a patch of landscape where the snow had gone and the grass hadn't yet arrived.

Then he looked at Phoebe and said, "Exploring by train? Nothing better!" His attention moved to Maggie, back to Phoebe, and then back to Maggie. He noticed Maggie's eyes seemed to smile warmly at him. *She's like a bird,* he thought. *Jittery. Nervous. Ready to fly.*

"Anything I want, Mom? Pancakes with huckleberry syrup?" Phoebe pleaded as she wiggled in her seat.

"Anything, Phoebe. As long as you drink all of your milk," Maggie said as she reached over and gently removed the locket of hair that had found its way down the center of Phoebe's forehead. As Maggie did so, her sleeve moved up, revealing a deep gash on her arm. Without meaning to, Jack found himself staring at it. *Those are quite the scratches you've got on your arm there, Maggie*, Jack thought. *Been wrestling with a bear?*

Chapter Five

Monday morning, 9 a.m.

Following Jack's eyes, Maggie quickly looked down at her arm with surprise and gently traced around the red gashes she noticed for the first time. She stared out the window, past Jack and all the other diners in the dining car. *On a train*, she thought, *it's as if you're standing still and the world is rushing by*. As she watched the evergreens speed past her, she traveled back to her first time on the train with her dad. She would've been Phoebe's age. She was staring out the window then too. "Dad," she remembered asking, "how come our train just veered to the right? It looks like we just left our track!" He had thought for a moment as he always did before answering. "It's called a railroad switch, Maggie. Did you see how the tracks split? The engineer pulls a lever, and the train moves from one track to the other, smoothly. Without notice. It's how a train changes direction."

Fascinating, young Maggie had thought. Mature Maggie wondered, *How can such a major change come from such a seemingly tiny action?* Life was like that, she figured. Hers anyway. Everything goes along, goes along, goes along, and then suddenly, everything is completely, utterly different. Almost without effort. Here she was on a train, leaving her entire world behind. All of it, of course, except the best part—Phoebe.

The moment Phoebe was born, Maggie knew everything had changed. She wasn't exactly sure how, and she wasn't convinced she was ready for it, but a different Maggie came out of the hospital on that clear, cold October morning. The air was biting, but Maggie felt warm. She wasn't alone. Matt was with her as usual. But having Phoebe in the world changed everything.

And in this particular moment, on the train with Phoebe safely beside her, everything seemed to be changing again.

"Mom, can I open this now? Please?" Maggie looked at the clear plastic bag filled with a tiny box of crayons and a few sheets to color. It wasn't much, but Maggie was grateful that the waiter had brought it along with the menus.

"Sure, honey."

"What do you have there, Phoebe?" asked Jack moments after the waiter took their order.

"Colors. And coloring pages," she answered proudly. "It's my goody bag. That guy just gave it to me."

"Nice!" was Jack's response. "I didn't get one." The corners of his mouth drooped down.

Maggie chuckled.

"I can share," Phoebe offered as she handed over a green crayon and a small sheet of paper with the outline of a train on it. "I have two pictures to color. And four crayons."

Maggie felt as if she were standing back, observing her daughter at a distance. Here Phoebe was, interacting with a stranger, with kindness and grace. *There's still hope*, she thought.

Jack carefully outlined his train in green, then filled it in with a softer shade by holding his crayon ever so lightly.

Maggie watched as Phoebe carefully studied Jack's technique.

"You're a very good colorer, Jack. Here, you can use the red one too. We can trade," explained Phoebe as she handed the red crayon to Jack.

"Thanks, Phoebe. What other colors do you have?" he asked.

"Blue and yellow. When you finish with the red, you can have blue. I have more crayons back at our seat, too." Phoebe carefully put the green crayon back in its box. She then pulled out the blue one and started to outline one of her trees, just like Jack had done.

When Jack and Phoebe were almost finished with their coloring, the waiter returned, holding a large tray. "Two orders of pancakes and an egg sandwich here," he announced.

"Time to put the colors away," said Maggie as she scooted the crayons and papers to the side to make room for breakfast.

Jack was the first to dig in, filling his fork with a heaping bite of pancakes. As he shoved the bite into his mouth, he managed to say, "These are delicious. How are yours, Phoebe?"

"So good." She smiled. Maggie was pleased that Phoebe's healthy appetite had returned. And that she had a new friend.

Before Maggie was halfway through with her egg sandwich, Phoebe's plate was empty. "Nice job, Phoebe," said Maggie.

Phoebe took a big swig of milk and smiled.

"Is that enough milk, Mommy? I'm full," said Phoebe, who now had huckleberry syrup dripping down her chin. "Do you want to play today, Jack?" she asked as she smiled over at her new friend.

"I would," he said. "I'm not too bad at tic-tac-toe. Have you ever played that?"

"I like tic-tac-toe," she replied.

"Maybe later we can play a game or two," he suggested. "Hang on to those crayons, Phoebe. We'll need them!"

"You can keep these. I have more," said Phoebe, as she looked over at her mom, with a pleading look. "Can I play with Jack again later, Mom?"

Maggie nodded and then wiped Phoebe's mouth off with her sleeve. Almost immediately, she jerked her hand away, as if she had been reprimanded. That internal voice inside her head had started up again. "What kind of mother does that? Wipes her kid's face with her sleeve? What's wrong with you?" She shook her head as if to shake away the voice that wasn't there. She picked up the napkin and finished cleaning up Phoebe's mouth. Properly.

"It's been a while since I've been on a train," said Jack, bringing Maggie back to the present moment. "I forgot how relaxing it is."

"I was just thinking that too. When was your last time?" she asked.

He thought for a minute. "I would've been about ten. A fishing trip with Sam."

Who is Sam? Maggie thought as she smiled.

"Sam is a family friend. He thought every ten-year boy should experience a train trip. He also believed every kid needed to know how to fish. So he accomplished both in one short weekend."

"That sounds like fun."

"Actually, it was a blast. He was one of the few cops in town. And I learned more about what I shouldn't do that weekend than any other time in my life. Up to that point anyway."

"I'm afraid to ask," said Maggie.

"Oh, harmless stuff mostly. Explosive bottle rockets, stuff like that. What about you, Maggie?"

"Same," she replied.

"Fishing trip with Sam?" Jack laughed.

"No, silly, I was about nine. With my dad. We traveled by train cross country. I loved it!"

"Family vacation?"

"No, we were moving. Heading west. My mom had died shortly before that. Think we were looking for a fresh start."

Jack nodded thoughtfully.

"Kind of impulsive of my dad," added Maggie. "I know he didn't have a job lined up. I'm not even sure he knew where we were going. But it all worked out. It usually does, I guess. I'm hoping it usually does. Right, Phoebe?"

Phoebe smiled, happy to be included in what felt like an adult conversation.

"Yeah, I'm hoping it does too," said Jack.

"You did quite well with your pancakes, young lady," said Maggie. "Thanks for sharing your table with us, Jack." Maggie nodded warmly to Jack as she and Phoebe stood up to leave.

"My pleasure. Maybe we'll meet again for lunch?" he said as he reached his hand out once again to shake Phoebe's.

"Yes, please," said Phoebe before her mom had a chance to respond.

Maggie smiled as she and Phoebe turned from the table and made their way back through the cars to their seats. *That was fun,* thought Maggie. *Nice guy.*

Maggie knew that within thirty minutes, Phoebe would be sound asleep. And Maggie would have a solid hour to get things done, if she were home. Typically, nap times were her most productive times of the day. But now, on this train, going nowhere in particular, Maggie had nothing to accomplish. Nothing to do except stare out the window and watch her world change direction right before her eyes.

Chapter Six

Monday morning, 9:40 a.m.

Jack slowly finished the rest of his pancakes, being careful to soak up every last drop of syrup. As usual, he had saved the most drenched bite for last. Being out hadn't been easy. He'd heard there would be challenges. Hard to get work, for one. He'd encountered that one already. As soon as he got out, he took the train to Sandpoint. "If you're going to find a job, Jack, it's a good place to start," his cell mate had told him. "They hire people like us." But after a full week of filling out applications at every gas station, diner, and convenience store that he could find, Jack hadn't managed to land even one interview. He'd expected that, though. It would just take time and a lot of effort. But there were other things he hadn't counted on, like the lack of structure. For four years now, someone else had been calling all the shots. When to wake up, what to eat, where to go, what to do. He had no say in any of it. And he'd adjusted to that. Amazing how the human spirit can adapt. Adjust. Survive. *It's what we do*, he thought. But this adjustment? More challenging than he'd anticipated. And the worst part, he had no one to talk to about it. Out here, he was on his own. And more alone than he'd ever been before.

In a day or two, I'll be at my mom's, he thought as he stood up and made his way out of the dining car. It was only half full now—the Monday morning breakfast crowd had dissipated. He wasn't ready to return to his seat, though, so he went in the opposite direction, wandering through a few more passenger cars. On his right, he observed a retired couple, maybe taking the cross-country trip they'd promised each other for decades. The man's face was hidden behind *The New York Times*, legs crossed, sipping coffee from a white Styrofoam cup. His wife sat motionless, her lap filled with projects to occupy her time, a half-made scarf, balls of yarn, and knitting needles. But her eyes were focused elsewhere, beyond the evergreen trees speeding by to the snow-capped mountains in the distance. Next, an elderly gentleman sitting alone, watching the family of five a few rows ahead of him, with three young boys fighting over an iPad. He smiled up at Jack as he passed by. Jack nodded. In the last row, in the last car, Jack found what he was looking for—an empty seat. Without knowing why, he settled in and stared out the window. He felt comfortable here, tucked away, unseen and unnoticed. And the rocking motion of the train did its magic as it lulled him to sleep.

Jack awoke suddenly, sat up abruptly, and looked around. He didn't sleep soundly anymore. He didn't imagine he ever would again. Always slightly vigilant. On guard. But there was no one around. Nothing to wake him but his own thoughts. Out the window, he noticed the sun had risen high above the mountains.

He must've been dreaming of his mother, he thought. He was feeling slightly agitated. Not about anything his mother had done, for sure. She wasn't at fault. But she would probably be dreading his visit, he reckoned. That's one of the reasons he hadn't told her he was coming. She didn't even know about his early release. Of all the people on earth, she'd seen the worst of him. And never said anything. If she had any fault in the matter, it would be that she had loved him too much—and didn't kick him out when she really should have.

Jack shook his head slowly and softly muttered, "I'm sorry." On the bright side, he honestly wasn't the man he once had been. In some respects, the last four years had been really good for Jack. *Eyes on the road ahead*, he told himself reassuringly. *The past is past; it's over. You're in a different place now.*

The train pulled into a station. Cut Bank, Montana. *Timeless*, thought Jack. Not too much had changed about train travel in Jack's lifetime. He stared out the window at the assortment of soon-to-be passengers eagerly awaiting the train's arrival. An elderly gentleman standing alone, holding a tattered briefcase, ripened to perfection. Two young men, in their mid-twenties, dressed in crisp new jeans and Carhartt jackets. A tall, slender woman with dirty blonde hair pulled back in a ponytail and a long black overcoat. This one, Jack realized, wasn't a stranger at all. It was Rebecca. His heart dropped a moment as he watched her survey the length of the train, trying to decide which car to enter. *Not this one*, thought Jack as he lowered his head in the unlikely event that she would notice him through the window.

Chapter Seven

Monday morning, 10:40 a.m.

Phoebe was sound asleep, her little head resting against her mom. Phoebe's arms were wrapped tightly around Mr. Snuggles, who was once bright pink but now was worn thin and pale from love. *Now*, thought Maggie, *would be the time to find some antibiotics for this cut on my arm*, as she rubbed her finger around the outside of the gash once again. She hadn't realized it was there until she had noticed Jack staring at it earlier. Now she was forced to think about it, about the moment. That old pitchfork out in the shed had been rusty, really rusty. But that hadn't been her biggest concern at the time. It hadn't been her concern at all, until this moment. Maggie looked down at Phoebe, who was snoring in a soft cooing way, and smiled. Maggie pulled an old comb out of her pocket and began to work it gently through Phoebe's tangled hair, humming softly to her as she slept.

As the train pulled into Cut Bank, Maggie wondered where these new passengers were headed. Only one had a suitcase, a rather expensive silver one on roller wheels, with a red sash tied around the handle. *For identification purposes*, thought Maggie. The woman attached to the suitcase was tall, with dirty blonde hair pulled back neatly into a ponytail. *She looks distracted*, thought Maggie. *Where is she going? Or what is she running from?* All the other people standing by her looked like day trippers. Heading somewhere, and then heading home. *Home. Now there's a word that doesn't bring up an image. One day*, Maggie promised herself, *Phoebe and I will have a home. A place that's ours. Just ours. Filled with dandelion bouquets and wooden toys and bookshelves stuffed with books. White lace curtains in the windows and classical music playing in the background.* Just the thought made Maggie smile as she looked up to see the woman in the long dark coat standing directly beside her.

"Is this seat taken?" the stranger asked as she pointed to Jack's empty seat.

Nudged out of her revelry, Maggie shook her head no, then quickly corrected herself. "Yes, there's a young man sitting there."

The woman looked around and then pointed to the empty seat directly in front of Maggie. "How about this one?" she asked.

"All yours," replied Maggie with a nod. The woman settled in quietly, taking off her long coat and storing her silver bag in the luggage compartment above the seat. Maggie returned her gaze to Phoebe's long blonde curls as she continued to work the comb through the knots that had found a home there.

Jolted out of her thoughts once again, Maggie heard the familiar bing of her cell phone. Instinctively, she glanced down to see who was trying to reach her, knowing full well it could be only one person. "WHERE THE HELL ARE YOU?" appeared beside Matt's picture. She quickly dropped her phone on the floor, trying to erase the impact it had on her newly acquired sense of peace. Her first response was to answer him, to keep him from getting angrier. Her eyes nervously darted around her, front to side, from side to back, and back to front again. But then she remembered he didn't know where she was. And as long as he didn't, she felt safe. Bending over to pick up her phone, she realized she had never really wanted a cell phone. Aside from Matt, who did she talk to? But he had insisted she have one, and that she carry it with her at all times. On their first anniversary, he had presented it to her as if it had been the present she had always longed for. "News apps, a flashlight, calculator, camera, weather information, even a complete library," he had told her. "This phone is everything you'll ever need." But everything Maggie needed was right here, in front of her, sleeping peacefully.

The front door to the train car swung open as the conductor made his way down the aisle.

"Tickets. Tickets, please," he bellowed again, as he leaned his body against the seat in front of Maggie. He reached his hand out to collect the ticket from the woman with the dirty blonde hair. Nodding to her, he answered, "Just shy of six hours," as if she'd asked him a question. With that, he looked at the seat behind, and smiled at the now waking Phoebe.

"Mom," said Phoebe. "I'm hungry!"

"Again?" asked Maggie, before realizing a few hours had passed. "Okay, let's go have lunch!"

Chapter Eight

Monday morning, 11:45 a.m.

"Excuse me, what time do you have?" Jack asked the elderly lady in front of him.

"Not quite noon," was the answer.

Jack stood up slowly, tugged his coat collar up, and lowered his eyes as he started rocking his way through the car. By wandering to the last car on the train and falling asleep, he'd managed to avoid Rebecca as she boarded the train. *I couldn't have planned that one better*, he thought. But he was hungry. And he couldn't keep running away forever. Just as he made his way to the dining-car door, he noticed Maggie and Phoebe making their way from the opposite end of the car. *Nice*, thought Jack. *They must be on the same schedule as I am.*

"Hi, Jack," chirped Phoebe as he came into her line of vision. "I just woke up!" Jack laughed. Even at a distance, he could see sleep lines etched into Phoebe's young face. "Mom says there's no better place to sleep than on a train."

"I agree," said Jack. "That's what I've been doing for most of the morning!" As the three of them waited for a table to clear, Jack looked across at Phoebe and thought this must be what it was like to belong. To have someone happy to see you. "And what about you, Maggie? What have you been doing?"

"Not a thing," Maggie replied, smiling. Unlike Phoebe, who looked well rested and fresh, Maggie looked a little stressed, thought Jack. *Something going on in there*, he speculated. He had quite a few questions, but he knew better than to pry. "You take what you're given"—that had always been his motto. And just this little bit of social interaction was a welcomed change for Jack. Before long, a table emptied and the three of them made their way to it.

"So what's for lunch, Ms. Phoebe?" Jack asked as he looked over the menu.

"I'm having a peanut butter and jelly sandwich," said Phoebe proudly. "That's Dad's favorite!"

"Where is your dad?" asked Jack, instantly wishing he could retract the question. He caught an irritated look wash over Maggie's face.

"Home," Maggie said. And to change the subject, she brought up a subject she typically tried to avoid: dessert. "A cookie after lunch?" she asked Phoebe.

"Oh, yes, Mom. I'll eat all my sandwich first," promised Phoebe.

"So Jack," asked Maggie, "tell us more about yourself. You're headed home to see your mom. Where have you been?"

Touché, thought Jack. "I've been away, as they say. Made some mistakes. Bad ones. And I've been learning from those. I guess you could say they sent me away to grow up." After a moment, he added, "I think it worked."

"Oh," said Maggie, a bit surprised by his honesty. "For a while?"

"Four years," he replied. Maggie wasn't the only one surprised by Jack's candor—he hadn't seen this openness coming either. But there it was, out on the table. If Jack hadn't been so surprised, he might've found the silence uncomfortable. But it afforded him a few moments to catch up with what had just happened. *Cool*, he thought. *Honesty*. It hadn't been his regular M.O. But he kind of liked it.

"I was four last year," said Phoebe, adding her two cents to the conversation. "But I'm five now."

"That's a pretty big number, Phoebe!" said Jack. He felt lighter. Much lighter. As the waitress came over to the table, Jack found himself ordering twice what he normally would have. And as he looked up and saw Rebecca enter the dining car, he didn't feel quite as sick to his stomach as he had thought he would.

Chapter Nine

Monday afternoon, 12:05 p.m.

Jack seems like an ordinary guy, thought Maggie. No rough edges or odd mannerisms. His face, though unshaven, was almost childlike. Innocent looking. And the way he related to Phoebe seemed so cute. Without being aware of it, Maggie scooted Phoebe just a little closer to her. *Doing time for what?* Maggie wondered. She studied him closely now. *He seemed almost relieved when he shared his little news with us*, she thought. *And now he looks like he might throw up.*

Maggie watched Jack's gaze as his eyes fixated on the dining car door. She turned to see what had caught his attention and noticed the tall woman with the ponytail standing there. "Oh, she just got on the train at the last stop. She's sitting across from you now. We could wave her over," said Maggie.

"I'd rather not," was all Jack could say, as he shifted his eyes downward to study his utensils.

Maggie's gut subtly nudged her. She wasn't always good at feeling the nudge, but this time, she got it. Her first thought was to take

Phoebe's hand and run. But something told her "stay." So she did. "Jack, I don't know you at all, but are you okay?" She looked up over Jack's head to the other side of the room again and noticed that the woman had left. "She probably couldn't find a seat and figured she'd come back later," muttered Maggie.

She watched as Jack looked up again and his face relaxed. "An old friend I'm just not ready to run into yet. She and I, we have some history," he said as he looked straight at Maggie and then at Phoebe. "I'll fill you in later if you're interested."

Here's a guy on a train with a record, running away from people, and I feel a strange kinship with him, Maggie mused. *Maybe we're not so different.* She'd always believed that some people come into your life, or pass through it, for a reason. Sometimes, they need to learn something, and you're the conduit; other times, it's the opposite. But something told Maggie "stay." And for once in her life, she decided to listen.

The rest of lunch was uneventful. As promised, Phoebe finished her sandwich. Jack did remarkably well, too. He devoured his entire turkey sandwich, chips, and even his pickle. Once the promised cookie was consumed and they were headed back to their seats, Maggie whispered to Jack, "Her seat is across from yours, you know."

He nodded. "Thanks for the heads up. I heard you say that. I just needed a few minutes before facing her."

Chapter Ten

Monday afternoon, 12:45 p.m.

As Jack reached his seat, he looked over at Rebecca. He wasn't sure whether she had seen him in the dining car, but she definitely saw him now. *No sign of a long lost friend on her face*, he thought. He gestured in such a way as if to ask if he could join her. And the answer was a cold hard stare. A moment of utter silence. Jack didn't move. There must've been a pleading look on his face because Rebecca motioned for him to sit down. "You've got one minute," she stated.

Jack sucked in a wallop of train-car air and began. "I'm sorry."

That was the hardest part. What followed just flowed. Maybe because it had been churning in his mind for four years now.

"I never meant for that to happen," he whispered. "Chad and I started the night at a party. Over on Dawson Street," he proceeded slowly. "As usual, we got wasted. And some pretty stupid ideas started flowing." Jack looked up and noticed that Rebecca was listening intently, with a hard stoic look.

"Go on."

"I don't even remember whose stupid idea it was," he said. "And it doesn't matter. I should've been looking out for Chad. I should've stopped it. I should've stopped us." Jack rested for a moment. Neither of them said anything for a few minutes. Jack handed Rebecca a tissue, which was actually the dinner napkin he had tucked into his pocket earlier. He had anticipated this moment. Had hoped for this moment. "It's my fault. And I'm sorry." He wasn't looking for forgiveness. How could Rebecca ever forgive him for being so irresponsible with her younger brother?

No, Jack realized, he was looking for something else. Something like freedom from those thoughts in the night that ate at his gut, night after night after night. He couldn't change what had happened that night; he knew that. But he could own it, apologize for it, and make sure something like that never happened again.

Rebecca didn't say a word. She kept her gaze down, away from Jack, and wiped away her tears. He sat silently beside her, careful not to touch her. Nothing more was said. Nothing more needed to be said. Rebecca eventually turned her head toward the window, letting Jack know the conversation was over. She'd heard what he'd had to say. Jack stood up and headed back to the dining car, where he ordered a cup of coffee. He sat there for half an hour, letting it grow cold. When he finally returned to his seat, Rebecca was gone.

Chapter Eleven

Monday afternoon, 1:00 p.m.

Maggie's eyes slowly opened as the train was coming into the station. What station, she wasn't sure. Didn't really matter, she realized. Her phone's screen brightened with another text message from Matt, demanding to know where she was. For all she knew, he was probably tracking her. Suddenly, she felt sick to her stomach. Of course he would be tracking her. Through her phone. Why hadn't she thought of this before? In the row in front of her, the woman with the long blonde ponytail was shuffling about, picking up her belongings. She'd set her silver roller bag down in the aisle, along with her handbag, waiting as the train slowly came to a stop. Maggie looked down at her phone again, wishing she could be free of Matt, once and for all. And why couldn't she? With one swift movement, she dropped her cell phone into the woman's bag.

Done, she thought proudly. The woman would find a strange phone in her bag and toss it. Matt would end up on a wild goose chase, with nothing to show for it. And she'd be free to start a new life. At least for a while. She looked over at a sleeping Phoebe, cuddled up in a ball, with Mr. Snuggles stuffed into her armpit. Phoebe stirred. Maggie rubbed her back for a few moments and then drifted back to sleep.

An hour later, as the afternoon sun lit the mountains in a soft, gentle way, Maggie woke from an early afternoon nap. No one else was awake; the world was hers. No pressing issues, no one who needed tending to. She felt peace. In an oddly symbolic way, passing her cell phone off to the stranger in the seat in front of her had eased her mind; she'd slept well these past sixty minutes. She felt rested.

What had happened, she wondered, these past five or so years? When did the constant criticism begin? Once, when Phoebe had been fussy, Maggie remembered trying everything—a bottle, a clean diaper. She had rocked her, held her, found her favorite pacifier. Nothing seemed to soothe Phoebe. But Phoebe's upset was nothing compared to Matt's. "This is all your fault!" he'd shout over the crying baby. "Can't you make her stop?" As a last resort, Maggie had bundled up Phoebe, put her in her car seat, and the two of them had driven for over an hour, through the downtown area of Whitefish, alive with activity. A few preseason shoppers, getting a jump on the holidays. Skiers celebrating a day on the slopes. Some business folk, bankers or lawyers probably, rounding off the evening. *A welcomed change*, Maggie had thought. By this time, Phoebe had settled down. "If it's all my fault," Maggie had reasoned, "then I can fix it."

And for years, she had tried.

Riding along next to Phoebe, Maggie thought back to a time when she was Phoebe's age.

"Maggie," her father sang out, "we've got a problem here. And we need to fix it!" Six-year-old Maggie came skipping downstairs. She loved a challenge, especially when it came from her father.

"What's up, Dad? Whatcha got?" She pulled on his arm to reach his hand.

"Here, follow me," he said as he led her out of the house, into the garage. He pointed to a flat tire on his truck's front passenger side and shook his head. Maggie nodded solemnly.

"That's broken, Dad. It's flat."

"That's right, Maggie. So what do we do about it this time?" he asked.

"Let's blow it up!" screamed Maggie. Her dad chuckled.

"Okay, Maggie, but what if there's a hole in it? Won't all the air come right out?" he asked.

"Maybe we better fix the hole first, Daddy," she suggested thoughtfully.

"Good idea, Maggie." He lifted her up and set her down on her special red stool, the one that twirled around. He softly hummed some old tune he was always humming when he worked in the garage. Maggie swung her legs back and forth on the stool, in time to his old tune, and watched carefully as her father continued to ask her what to do next. There was no better way to spend a Sunday afternoon, thought Maggie. Sometimes, she even hoped for flat tires or broken shutters—any challenge, as long as she could tackle it with her dad.

"Who can fix this?" he'd ask.

"We can!" they'd sing out together. "Maggie and her daddy. That's who!"

Chapter Twelve

Monday afternoon, 1:00 p.m.

Okay, this was not only awkward, it was painful, thought Rebecca as she looked over at Jack's empty seat after he wandered off. She didn't want to forgive him. She knew he'd suffered plenty. And done time. Spent four years in jail. But if she forgave him, she'd have nothing to focus all her anger on.

It's so much easier to get angry than to feel sad, she thought. She missed Chad. If she allowed herself to feel the sadness inside of her, she'd get lost in it. She wouldn't be able to find her way out. Anger, on the other hand, was directed outward, at someone else.

The train slowed as it entered the station. "Havre—Havre, Montana," announced the conductor as the train came to a stop. *I need to get out of here,* thought Rebecca as she grabbed her overnight bag and set it in the aisle. She never would have gotten on this train if she'd thought she would have even the slightest chance of running into Jack. She could've just as easily driven to her parents' house. Why was he here? How did he get out early? Why had no one mentioned this? Rebecca stood, put her jacket on, slung her handbag over her shoulder, and grabbed her overnight bag.

Rebecca stepped off the train. *I have to get out of here,* she repeated to herself. Once safely off the train, she took a deep breath. *Okay, Becca,* she said to herself, *now what? Facts. You have to get home. Mom and Dad are expecting you. Today.* She took three more deep breaths. *The next train isn't until tomorrow. Staying in Havre isn't an option. So, I get back on the train,* she thought reluctantly. After one more deep breath, she marched resolutely down the entire length of the train and boarded the last car. Empty seats everywhere, she thought as she made her way to the last seat and settled in for the remainder of her trip.

Chapter Thirteen

Monday afternoon, 1:30 p.m.

When Jack returned to his seat, he let his tall, lean body collapse into the worn cushions of the train. He breathed out deeply, releasing years' worth of stored tension. Rebecca was gone. All traces of Rebecca were gone. It was as if she'd never been there, except Jack felt immensely lighter. *Odd how you just kind of run into the people you need to make amends to*, thought Jack. He'd heard that actually happens a lot. *However it works, it seems to be working*, he thought. Maybe he'd spent enough time beating himself up. Four years is a long time to live in hell.

It had been a typical night. Jack would've just turned eighteen. And his goal, as usual—to get wasted. He'd wandered over to Rebecca's house, knowing beforehand she'd wind up hanging with her friends rather than doing anything with Jack. She never did anything with Jack. Jack was Jack. Too immature. Not serious enough for Rebecca. And most important, two years younger. But that never seemed to stop him from wandering over and giving it a shot. In fact, that was how he and Chad had become friends.

"She's not going out with you tonight either," said Chad, laughing. "Man, you just keep coming back for more."

"Whatever," was Jack's response. But not his attitude. He really did like Rebecca. What was it about her? Unlike most of the people Jack had ever met, Rebecca didn't do anything to look good or to make other people like her. She would do something because it was the right thing to do. And that was something Jack hadn't seen a lot of. It was some kind of strength of character, he figured. She didn't appear strong, though. Not physically. In fact, she was a full head shorter than Chad, her baby brother by three years. She was petite like a little petunia, as her dad would say. But she was one of those people you didn't want to mess with, and Jack knew this. He loved her for it, too.

One day in junior high, a group of kids were picking on Nathan, a friend of Jack's. It was just before the morning bell, in the park right across from the school. As Jack's bus pulled up front, he watched as these three kids had Nathan cornered, backed up against the fence. Nathan was scared. Jack could see that. He was hunched over, his little body shaking.

What the hell? thought Jack. *What are they doing? Trying to get his homework?* All they'd have to do was ask. Nathan was a nice kid. He'd do anything for anybody. But Jack knew they probably didn't give a crap about his homework. Creeps like that just wanted to feel big. Jack shook his head. What could he do about it? *Not really my business*, he told himself. But he kind of knew it was. As he was wrestling with his conscience—*Do I step in and risk looking stupid or getting hurt? Or stay out of it, and feel like a shit for not helping my friend*—he noticed Rebecca. She was one seat in front of him on the bus. Up she stood, grabbed her backpack, and headed to the bus door before the bus had come to a stop. "Out!" she commanded the bus driver. And within seconds, she was across the grass, standing face to face with all three of those jerks. She didn't say much. She didn't have to. "This is not okay." She didn't back down. Not even an inch. She stared them directly in the eyes. Finally, they picked up their backpacks and walked away. Granted, she was a few years older than them. But still, it never happened again. Not to Nathan.

Jack wished she'd hang out with him and Chad sometime. But he never told Chad that.

Anyway, on this particular night, it was business as usual. After Rebecca and her friend departed, Jack and Chad grabbed a fifth of vodka from Chad's parents' liquor cabinet, poured most of it into a thirty-two-ounce plastic water bottle, and filled the now mostly empty liquor bottle back up with water. A good start, Jack remembered thinking, as they headed out on a night that would alter their lives forever.

Thinking back now, Jack realized he had never meant for any of it to happen. He never thought about the consequences. Never thought about anything except getting that next drink. Once he started, that's what he did. Alcohol or beer or vodka, whatever it was, it let him explode. All his inhibitions dissolved. He has able to let loose. Completely. Somehow, a few good swigs and he felt on top of the world. Invincible. Unstoppable. It was almost like a rocket being set off—destination unknown. And unimportant.

As the night's plans started to take shape, that all-too-familiar excitement started rolling inside of Jack. "We'll head to the party. We'll get some more liquor on our way." *Even acquiring our liquor was part of the intoxication*, Jack remembered. Chad wasn't of age, and Jack wasn't of means. They were resourceful, though. *Just because we didn't have any, and couldn't afford any*, Jack recalled, *never meant we weren't going to get any.*

Darkness set in. The two of them wandered over to Custer Street, which had become one of the quieter streets in Wolf Point. Most of the kids a few years ahead of Jack had moved away, and their parents had settled into a sedentary life of nothingness. Chad and Jack, they were the only creatures moving on that street that night. And they weren't being all too quiet, as Jack remembered. Chad was going on and on about something that had happened at school earlier that day. How Ms. Engels had the hots for him; he was sure of it. According to Chad, that lady was always giving him the eye and offering him extra credit, among other things. And one of these days, Chad swore, he was going to give that bitch what she was asking for. Jack nodded with a trace of skepticism that went totally unnoticed by Chad.

They trudged along Custer Street, checking out the houses, Jack mostly listening to Chad's near conquests with women. That's when they came up to the big old gray house where the Roberts lived. Mr. Roberts was hardly ever home, and the kids were gone. They'd been gone for years. And Mrs. Roberts, she was usually drunk or stoned or something. No one hardly ever saw her around the house or around town. She'd once been head of the PTA or something like that. Up in everybody's business. But now, nothing. Just fading away.

"Hey, man, I bet that door to the garage is unlocked," said Chad as they approached the Roberts' driveway.

"Bet you're right," Jack replied as the two of them sauntered toward the house. No lights came on. Perfect. Jack knew the amount of vodka remaining in their water bottle wasn't going to be enough for the night so it was time to go "shopping," as they called it.

Chad tried the door on the far side of the garage. "Bingo!" called Chad, giving Jack the thumbs-up sign. "We're in!" Chad entered the garage first. He had an uncanny way of locating the stash. For some reason, he could find the wine bottles, beer cans, or liquor being stored in any garage. Quickly, too. Jack just stood back and watched Chad do his magic. And he kept a lookout for unwanted obstacles like the homeowners. Or a passing police car. To date, Jack and Chad had been lucky. Dozens of "shopping trips," and not even a close call. Nothing. *There just wasn't a better way to get the goods*, thought Jack.

"What's your preference, sir?" asked Chad. "Tonight's selection includes bourbon, whiskey or gin." Just as Jack was about to answer, the door to the house swung open. "What the hell...?" and the sound of a gun being cocked.

"Run!" screamed Jack, as he turned and bolted out the side door. Chad dropped the liquor bottle he was holding. It shattered all around his feet. As he turned to flee, he stumbled over a trash can. He pulled himself up just as the gun fired.

"Shit!" screamed Chad as he pissed his pants and scurried out the garage door, lunging into the bushes to catch his breath.

Lights flooded the house's exterior, one turning on right after another. The sound of the gun cocking again filled the air. Chad lay motionless in the grass, behind the hedge. He didn't move an inch.

"You little shits!" screamed a gruff, smoke-filled voice. "You're not stealing from me again!" The woman fired her gun into the hedge. "Not this house. Not tonight," she muttered as she cocked the gun again. She was probably sixty years old, but she could easily be mistaken for a crazed old witch. Her hair was standing straight up from all sides. Kind of like a dead dandelion. Draped over her shoulders was a tattered, pink, flowered bathrobe. And combat boots on her feet. What really stood out, though, was the old shotgun that seemed to be pointed straight at Chad.

Out of nowhere, a bottle rocketed past her and shattered on the side of the house just behind her head. She turned around to investigate, dropping the gun by her side. Jack snuck quietly up to Chad and started tugging on the leg of his pants. He pressed his forefinger to his mouth. "Shh. Let's go," he whispered. Without looking back, the two ran as fast as they could through the backyard, jumping the chain-link fence, and disappearing in the overgrown park behind the Roberts' house.

"You smell like piss!" said Jack as he pulled himself up from the dirt pile where they'd landed.

"No shit, Jack. That bitch almost killed me!" Chad replied.

"She came pretty close," Jack agreed, starting to laugh. Wasn't he just congratulating himself on the two of them never running into such an encounter? Fortunately for them, Mrs. Roberts was probably four drinks into the evening so her aim was off. Chad stared at Jack, who was laughing almost uncontrollably now. The laughter proved contagious as Chad started laughing as well, crying so hard at the thought of Mrs. Rogers in her combat boots, firing away at Chad.

"Thanks, man. I owe you one," said Chad in a moment of appreciation.

"Yeah, and a bottle of whiskey." Jack laughed as the two of them got up and started walking again.

So now what? Jack remembered thinking. *We're not exactly off to a great start here. No more alcohol. We've been shot at. And Chad smells like piss.*

"Yeah, now what, mastermind?" asked Chad. "I'm thinking a change of clothes might be in order." Chad laughed. "I stink!"

"Okay, first things first. Priorities," said Jack, deciding to try to focus. "How to secure some more booze." Just because one attempt failed—what was it his dad used to say? "If at first you don't succeed…." Something like that. Jack had managed to fail at a number of things in his life, but acquiring alcohol was not one of them.

"Let's head back to your house. Get you some piss-free pants," said Jack. "Then we'll do this night right!"

By the time they reached Chad's house, no one was home, not even Chad's parents. Chad ran upstairs to change his pants while Jack made himself at home. Turkey sandwich, potato chips, and, of course, a dill pickle. To top it off, two shots of bourbon. Jack was in heaven. By the time Chad was back downstairs and ready to go, Jack was feeling happy. He didn't always find time for such an elaborate, well-cooked meal as a turkey sandwich. He laughed to himself. *It's the simple things that make all the difference*, Jack thought.

"Let's go, man. It's late enough already," Chad called to Jack as he grabbed a denim jacket.

"Where to now, Chad? We're kind of late for the party," said Jack as they headed out the door.

"Well, I'm thinking we'll borrow my dad's car," said Chad. "He's gone this weekend. He won't be needing it."

"Chad, you don't even have your license, dumb shit!"

"But I know how to drive. Dad lets me drive all the time."

"Whatever," said Jack as he headed to the driveway where an old '55 Chevy was parked. Chad's dad had recently restored this candy apple red Chevy back to the original hot rod he had raced a few decades earlier in high school. *Now this is a sweet ride*, thought Jack. He'd never before ridden in such a hot car.

As they got in the car, the same question came up. "And where are we going to get our booze now?"

"What about the Clarks over on Higgins? They're always good for a six pack or something," said Chad.

"Sounds good to me," Jack replied. After driving through a few quiet streets in a newer neighborhood, Chad pulled up to a curb, across the street and two houses down from a newer white ranch-style house. Inside, a few lights were on, making this one a bit more challenging than the last.

"Your turn, buddy," said Chad as he turned off the lights but kept the engine running. Jack slowly stepped out of the car, then watchfully crossed the street. Less than five minutes later, he returned with a big-ass grin on his face and two fifths, one in each hand.

As Jack recalled, the night proceeded as you might expect. At one point, he and Chad were at a friend's house with a bunch of kids who were still in high school. There was lots of sloppy drinking. Some immature flirting. A little dancing. And more sloppy drinking. Jack remembered putting his head into his hands, feeling the living room spinning round and round. That wasn't the feeling he was aiming for. Somehow, he always overshot the mark. A nice buzz, not giving a shit about anything, being on top of the world— those were his goals. But more times than not, he'd end up praying to the porcelain god, as they say. Or even worse, he'd wake up in some strange place, with no recollection at all of how he got there. Or what he had done. Or said to anyone. No memory. And a ton of woulda, coulda, shoulda. But all the regret in the world wasn't enough to get him to stop. Or rather, to get him not to start drinking the next time. It was what he did. It was who he was. And the consequences somehow weren't as bad as the thought of not doing it again.

The last thing Jack remembered from that night was a snapshot glimpse of the old Chevy and having to hang his head outside the window, trying not to get vomit all over the side of Chad's dad's pride and joy.

The next morning, Jack woke to a throbbing headache. In a place unfamiliar. As his brain started to process this new environment, he realized he was in a cage, behind bars, in a cell, on a cold, hard bench. That was bad enough, but he was also alone.

"What the hell," Jack muttered as he tried to piece together last night. This ending was definitely a new one. And where the hell was Chad? No one else was around. It was just Jack. He lay on the bench and thought. "I remember dancing," he whispered out loud. "I remember a house filled with people. I vaguely remember throwing up out the window. But how did I get here?"

⊞⊞⊞⊞⊞⊞⊞⊞⊞

It would be hours before Jack's question was answered. Eventually, his mom showed up. It was always his mom, bailing him out, coming to his rescue. Usually, it meant a silent scolding. Or just silence. This time was different, though. Jack could tell instantly. And it was bigger than just her son spending the night in jail, which wasn't a first for Jack. Her swollen red eyes met his bloodshot ones. And without a single word of greeting, she said to her only son, "What in the hell have you done this time, Jack?" Jack didn't know, but he knew enough not to say a word. He dove deep into her eyes, searching for the answer to her question, but none was there. Or it was too deep, too far from his reach. He would have to be patient. He would have to wait to learn what she already knew.

And now, four years later, on a train, in the middle of nowhere, Jack had run into Rebecca again. It had been four years since he'd seen Rebecca or his mom or anyone he'd grown up with. It had been four years since he'd had a drink or a drug. And it had been four years since the moment when Chad's body had to be pried out of his father's prized Chevy. Memories of that night never fully returned to Jack, just snippets at best, flashes or moments that might've actually happened or maybe didn't. Jack would never know. He vaguely remembered clutching Chad's hand to comfort him, only to discover that Chad's hand was no longer connected to his body. It had been severed. By glass maybe. And blood. There had been lots of blood.

And then nothing else. Nothing until the moment he woke up in jail, wondering what in the hell had happened.

Felony charges and four-years' time later, Rebecca still blamed Jack. Jack blamed Jack. If he hadn't dragged Chad along that night, if he hadn't been such a drunk little shit, maybe Chad would be here today. With Rebecca. And Jack would have a severed hand and be lying in a coffin somewhere. And that would be fine with Jack.

"Look who's feeling sorry for himself," Jack scolded as he snapped out of it. "Can't change the past. Can't see the future. You're here, buddy. This is all we get."

Chapter Fourteen

Monday afternoon, 1:35 p.m.

As Phoebe napped, Maggie stood, stretched, and then meandered over to where Jack was sitting.

"Hi," she said.

"Hello," he said, surprised to see her.

"Mind if I join you?" *A bit bold, don't you think, Maggie?* she asked herself. But she wanted to know more about Jack. He was becoming fast friends with Phoebe after all. She needed to know more. That's what she told herself anyway, which was part of the truth.

Jack nodded and motioned to the empty seat next to him. She sat. Silence filled the space between them. Then Maggie dove right in.

"I know it's none of my business, but what's the story with that lady?"

Without hesitation, Jack replied, "She's the sister of an old friend of mine."

"What's the unfinished business you mentioned at dinner? It seemed serious?" Maggie was surprised by her own directness.

Unbothered by the question, Jack continued to answer in a matter-of-fact manner. "I'm responsible for her brother's death."

"Oh," said Maggie.

After a moment, Jack continued: "A drunk-driving accident. My fault. I never got the chance to apologize to Rebecca." For Jack, coming clean meant more than just not drinking. It really was a matter of coming clean, no matter how hard that was. His eyes got a bit red and moist around the edges. Maggie could see the pain her questions were causing. She was sorry she'd pried. But not enough to stop.

"Is that why you've been in prison?" she asked.

"Yeah, four years."

"That's a long time," she said.

"Not enough, honestly. I got to walk away. My friend didn't. So, in some respects, I got off easy. He got the lifetime sentence."

Maggie didn't know what to say. Neither of them said a word for a good five minutes.

"No drink or drugs since," said Jack. "Not even once."

"I would think not—being locked up," she muttered.

"You'd be surprised what you can get your hands on inside. Couldn't tell you how many times I turned both down. It's every-where in there."

"What was it like—prison?" Maggie asked. Now she was curious. She'd never met anyone who'd spent any time in jail before. And Jack didn't seem to mind answering her questions.

"Kind of what you'd expect. Too much time. None of it yours. There's TV and meetings. Friendships of sorts. A different kind of friendship honestly."

"Not so horrible?" she asked.

"Hard to explain. You start to get used to it."

"What do you mean?"

"The routine. The lack of freedom. Everything being taken care of. Then getting out becomes a little hard."

"How so?"

"You're not really prepared to step back in. I was a kid when I went away. For the past four years, I've followed a set of rules that don't really apply anymore. There isn't any structure out here. My people are still in there. I'm out here alone trying to clean up my mess and pick up where I left off, which is completely impossible. There's no reset button. No do-overs. It's all just weird."

They both sat quietly. Maggie wasn't sure what to say, so she said nothing. She considered holding his hand, comforting him in some way, but that would've been weird. The silence that surrounded them was a comfortable silence, though, where nothing really needed to be said. Or done. Sitting quietly felt okay. Even necessary. Ironically, Maggie realized, sometimes space created closeness.

After a few minutes, Jack said, "I've spilt my guts. I think it's your turn now." Playfully, he added, "I've got a few questions for you."

Maggie looked at Jack and thought, *I could just sit here and tell him almost anything. Is it because he's a good listener? Or because I'll never see him again?* She wasn't sure. Kind of funny, though. Life on a train.

"Did you ever just run away?" asked Maggie. "Just up and go?"

"Not intentionally," said Jack. "I guess I used to have my own way of checking out when I needed to. Is that what you did, Maggie? Up and run?"

Maggie continued as if she hadn't heard a word he'd said. "Have things ever gotten bad and it's your fault? And you can't figure out how to fix 'em, so you just run?"

Jack was quiet for a moment. "You know, I went to a lot of group sessions in prison. They kind of helped me learn how to deal with life on life's terms."

"What do you mean?"

"Well, if I run from something, it tends to follow me. It gets bigger and bigger and bigger until it eats me alive."

"Whoa," said Maggie. "Glad I don't have that problem." She picked up one of Jack's crayons from breakfast and drew a picture of a great big green monster chasing a stick figure.

"Yeah, something like that," Jack said as he poked Maggie in the arm.

They sat quietly for a moment.

"No, seriously, though," said Jack, "I'm learning that if something's bothering me, I got to talk about it. And then I've got to deal with it. That's the only way around it—right through the middle of it."

She listened. *He sounds just like my dad*, Maggie thought, shaking her head. Some problems are just too big and ugly to deal with.

"Mom," the coming-to-consciousness voice of a five-year-old squeaked from one row back, across the aisle.

"I'm right here, Phoebe." Maggie stood up and stepped across the aisle. "Come join us—me and Jack," she said as she lifted Phoebe and cradled her like an oversized baby. Maggie sat down again beside Jack, and she turned Phoebe around so she was facing Jack.

"Hi, Jack," said Phoebe.

"Hi, Phoebe. How was your nap?"

"Bumpy. When do I get to sleep in my bed again? I miss my bed, Mom."

"Not too much longer, baby. We'll stop soon. We'll find a nice place to live, with a good school that you'll get to go to. How does that sound?"

"I like that," said Phoebe, not really understanding what was going on, but she seemed to be adjusting well. As long as she had her mom and Mr. Snuggles, all was good, or at least good enough.

"Jack, you mind watching Phoebe for a minute so I can run to the bathroom?" asked Maggie as she stood and stretched.

"Not at all," said Jack. He smiled at Phoebe.

"Hey, Jack," Phoebe asked, "want to play tic-tac-toe now?"

"You betcha," said Jack. "I used to be pretty good in my day." Phoebe pulled out her little pad of paper with two crayons, green for Jack and red for herself.

"You get green because, well, because I get red!" she said, as if that was all the explanation needed.

"That's my favorite color, Phoebe! I like green!"

Phoebe smiled. "Red's mine."

"Are you in school, Phoebe?" Jack asked.

"Not right now," she said. "I'm on a train, silly."

Jack laughed. "Yeah, true. But do you go to school?"

"Yeah, I'm in Kindergarten," said Phoebe. "I can write my name." She proudly scribbled across the top of the pad. "But we're going someplace new now, so I get a new school."

"What's your favorite part of school?" Jack asked as he marked his first green X.

"Well, I like lunch. And recess is good too," said Phoebe as she concentrated fiercely on the sheet of paper in front of her. "There!" she said as she strategically placed her red O. "Coloring is good, too. We don't get to do that a lot, though. And we never get to play tic-tac-toe."

Jack marked his second green X directly above Phoebe's O. She countered. His third landed in the far left spot.

"I won!" screamed Phoebe as she placed her third O right in a row.

"Yes, you did, Phoebe!" said Jack, excited for what seemed like her first tic-tac-toe victory ever.

Just then, Maggie returned.

"Phoebe and I were just playing a ruthless game of tic-tac-toe," Jack told her.

"Mind if I join you?" asked Maggie as she lifted Phoebe up, sat down by Jack, and set Phoebe on her lap.

"Not at all," Jack replied. "Phoebe was just telling me you're moving to a new home and she's starting a new school. That's exciting! I'm a little familiar with this area. Which town?" asked Jack.

Jack was direct. Straight up. To the point. Maggie would give him that. None of this hidden agenda approach that she'd grown so used to.

She wished she could answer his question. A simple "I don't know" didn't seem adequate. But instead, she said nothing.

The more Maggie talked to Jack, the more he reminded her of her father. Okay, maybe a version of her father who might have turned left when he should have gone right. But at heart, Jack seemed like a good man trying to be a better one.

"Hello, Maggie; you in there?" Jack asked again, waiting for a response.

Phoebe giggled.

"If it's Glasgow," Jack said, "then that's cool. That's a solid little town. I lived there for a few years when I was about your age, Phoebe. Nice park and an easy walk to the river. And good fishing." Jack nodded. "Decent school, too. At least that's what everyone says." He winked at Phoebe.

"How far is Glasgow from here?" asked Maggie.

"It might be the next stop. Or the one after," said Jack. He was starting to sense that Maggie had no idea where she was going.

"My mom's just an hour or so beyond Glasgow," Jack said. "That's where I'm headed. Slowly. Taking my time."

"Yeah," Maggie replied slowly. "Glasgow is where we're headed. I'm hoping to get a job. Find a little place." Maggie smiled and patted Phoebe's back a few times

Phoebe quietly, thoughtfully repeated the word, "Glasgow. Glasgow. Glasgow," as if trying out the name of her new home for the first time.

Jack looked at Maggie with a sly smile on his face.

"This has been in the plans for a while, huh, Maggie." He winked at her and nudged her on the arm.

"Okay, yeah, sure," she said. "About thirty seconds." She laughed. He laughed in response.

"I've got a little unfinished business there myself," muttered Jack. "Hey, if you guys don't mind, I might get off with you. I could help you find your way around before heading off to my mum's."

Jack was the closest thing to a friend Maggie had, ex-con or not, he was it, so she said, "Okay, and then you'll get back on the train and head to your mom's?"

"Yeah, just a quick stop for me."

"That sounds good, Jack. Thank you!"

Just then, the conductor came waltzing through, punching tickets along the way.

"How long 'til Glasgow?" asked Maggie.

"Not this stop. The one after. You've got about an hour and a half to go," was the prompt, courteous answer.

"Thank you," Maggie replied. As soon as the conductor was gone, she turned to Jack.

"I overheard a bit of the conversation you just had. With that lady. None of my business, but I admire how open and honest you were."

"Thanks, Maggie. I can assure you I haven't always been that way. I'm a work in progress, trying to be a better man than I used to be. That's my plan, anyway. That's my only plan."

"Sounds like a good one to me," said Maggie as she settled in comfortably for more rhythmic rocking on the train.

Chapter Fifteen

Monday afternoon, 2:45 p.m.

There was something so familiar about Maggie. It was as if Jack could see a part of himself in her childlike reaction to the world.

She'd fallen asleep again, this time on him, leaning on his shoulder, sitting on this train, running from something. He assumed she felt it too. She felt safe enough to let down her guard with him, a total stranger. But not a stranger at all. They had connected in a way he never had before. Without words.

He played with her hair and made her an unspoken promise. *Maggie, I got you. I got your back.* And somehow, he knew that she knew.

An hour later, Maggie woke up, a bit confused, sleeping on Jack's shoulder. Phoebe was stretched out on the seat opposite, sleeping peacefully with Mr. Snuggles. Maggie looked up, and Jack smiled at her. "She's fine," he said. "Hasn't woken up once."

Maggie pulled herself up slowly. "Sorry, Jack. Didn't mean to drool all over you."

He laughed. "You're good. I think you needed a solid nap."

She sat up and brushed her hair through with her fingers. Neither of them said a word. They just sat there, contently. Within minutes, Phoebe started to stir. She sat up, looked around, and smiled.

"Hi, Mom," she said. "Hi, Jack." By now she was standing, right in front of them. She hopped onto Maggie's lap, curled into a little ball like a kitten, and smiled.

"Meow," she purred. "Guess who I am?"

"You're mighty cute. You must be Spunky," guessed Maggie.

"Yep," Phoebe said.

"Spunky?" asked Jack.

"Spunky was our little kitty," said Phoebe. "He ran away. And then he came home dead."

"Oh, I'm sorry," said Jack.

"Yeah, it was sad. Mom cried."

"Remember how he used to purr?" asked Maggie.

"Like this?" asked Jack. He started purring ridiculously.

Phoebe laughed. "No silly. Like this." She purred softly.

"Okay, goofy girl," said Maggie. "How about we go walk around a bit? Stretch our legs. Won't be long before we get to our station so we'd better get you cleaned up a bit."

"Okay, Mommy. I'm going to miss this train. I like it."

"Me too, Phoebe," said Maggie, and off they went, bobbing and weaving down the aisle.

"Next stop, Glasgow!" sang the conductor as the train car door swung open. "Five minutes," he added as he nodded to Maggie. Maggie set Phoebe down and stood up. "You coming, Jack?"

"You betcha," was his answer.

Because right now, at this point in his life, he felt closer to these two strangers than to anyone else on earth. He really wasn't in a hurry to get to his mum's either. He was hoping he would have a job lined up elsewhere, like Sandpoint, before she even knew he was coming. That way, he could show up unannounced, make his apologies, and then get out of town fast—before anyone else found out he was there. An extra day or two with Maggie and Phoebe would be a welcomed delay from the inevitable.

Jack reached his long arms up overhead into the luggage bin and pulled out an old green duffle bag, home to a half-dozen T-shirts, two pairs of jeans, some clean underwear, one pair of socks, and an old shaving kit. These were his worldly possessions. He looked over to where Maggie and Phoebe were standing and noticed just their small overnight bag, nothing else.

"You ladies travel light, too," he said with a smile.

This should be interesting, thought Jack. *The three of us are like fugitives, running from our pasts. I can't remember mine, and I have no idea what theirs is. But whatever they are running from, it doesn't seem right.*

So Glasgow it is, thought Jack as the train slowly came to a screeching halt. He graciously nodded toward Maggie and Phoebe, indicating they should go first and he'd follow. And in that moment, the three travelers stepped off the train and into a new chapter of their lives.

Chapter Sixteen

Monday afternoon, 3:40 p.m.

Glasgow. Never even heard of it, thought Maggie as she led the way off the train, holding tightly to Phoebe's little hand. *Cute train station*, she thought, as she hoisted the backpack up on her shoulder. Phoebe seemed excited. *Life on a train is an amazing adventure for maybe a day or two*, thought Maggie. *But that's enough.* As she approached the front door of the station, Maggie stopped and started to panic. *What am I doing here? How am I going to make this work?* She breathed deeply. *What choice do you have, Maggie?"* she asked herself. As she took the next step into the station, she heard her father say, "Can't go left? Go right. Can't go back? Go forward!"

"Mom?"

"Yes, Phoebe?"

"Where are we going?"

"Well, we're going to get a bite to eat," said Maggie. "I bet you're hungry."

"I am hungry, Mom. I could eat all the blueberry pancakes in the world." Phoebe's world: What's for snack? When's dinner? And where's Mr. Snuggles? That was all Phoebe needed to know.

As they turned the corner, they saw a little diner, exactly what one might expect in a little town such as this. One block from the train station and next door to the hardware store. Maggie smiled. *Life here seems uncomplicated,* she thought. *Life here seems perfect.*

"You hungry, Jack?" Maggie asked as she looked at this strange guy from the train.

"Always," he replied.

A familiar stranger, thought Maggie.

"Glad to see the diner's still here," said Jack.

The three travelers quickly found a small table near the front. *Busy,* thought Maggie, *for such a small town. And in the middle of the afternoon. Lots of people! But not a lot of waitresses!*

The diner was straight out of the 1950s. Little posters and signs littered the walls, probably each one coated with a few decades of dust. *A warm family feel,* thought Maggie.

After a plate of French fries and an oversized chocolate chip cookie, Maggie asked the waitress if they were hiring.

"Does it snow in Montana in winter, honey?" was the response. "Hold tight, and I'll bring you an app. And not the kind you've got on your phone." She chuckled and walked off. She returned to the table with a coffeepot in one hand, a bill and an application in the other. "Fill it out now, and we'll have you filling up coffee cups in the morning!" She was mid-forties. Round. And someone who loved nothing better than talking with her neighbors all day long.

"So long, Burt. See you tomorrow!" she called out as one of the regulars hopped down from the stool at the counter and made his way to the door. She pulled her pen out from behind her ear, totaled up their check, and handed the pen to Maggie. "We are always hiring…if it's the right person," she said as she winked at Phoebe.

"I like it here, Mom. These French fries are the best," said Phoebe, with ketchup visible in both corners of her mouth.

Maggie looked over the application. Half-a-dozen questions, tops. It didn't even ask for references. *This is what I love about small town America. No one really cares where I came from.* She filled in her name, her maiden name actually. The date. Her availability. And the last question—past employment. She stopped for a moment and lifted her eyes from the application. Somehow, that would place her a little too close to home. She shivered. Past employment that's similar to this position, she rationalized. Then jotted down the names of both restaurants she'd worked at when she was in college in Virginia. *I'm guessing the only truth that really matters here is whether or not I can serve food. And that's something I'm quite good at.*

She set the blue ballpoint pen down and looked up again. "Maybe we should check out the school, Phoebe." *And a place to live*, thought Maggie. "This is such a cute town, Jack. How long did you live here?"

"Just a year or two," said Jack. "A good little town, as far as little towns go. Let's finish up here and wander around. See what else is still around."

Maggie picked up the pen again and signed the bottom of the application. "OK, guys, let's go!" she said as she stood up. She buttoned Phoebe's coat to the top, knowing they'd be wandering around town a bit.

"My name is Maggie," she offered as she handed her application over to the waitress, who was now the cashier.

"I'm Sally," said the waitress. "Would love to have you join us. We sure could use the help!"

"I might need a day," said Maggie, laughing. "We just got off the train and need to find a place to stay."

"Check the board at the community center," said Sally. "It's filled with rentals and part-time work for your guy there. Everything you'd need. The school is right across the street from the center too." She smiled. "You look smart enough to be in the first grade," Sally said to Phoebe as she bent down to meet her eye to eye.

"Kindergarten!" exclaimed Phoebe proudly. "I can write my name!"

Sally's eyes grew big to show she was impressed. The bigger her eyes grew, the more Maggie liked her.

"You might stop by the school first. To get this sweetie here enrolled. The school office closes at five o'clock, straight up," added Sally.

"Oh, good. Thank you," replied Maggie.

Sally briefly glanced at the application. "Okay, consider yourself hired, Maggie."

"Awesome. Thank you, Sally," Maggie said with a smile as the three of them headed out the door and into their new little world.

The late afternoon sun was shining, but the wind struck their faces like a cold, harsh slap. Maggie zipped up Phoebe's coat as they walked down the sidewalk. Up ahead to the right was the elementary school and to the left the community center.

"How 'bout we meet you at the community center just as soon as we're done, Jack?" asked Maggie as she pointed in the direction of the school. "It's not quite five o'clock yet, so we've still got a shot at getting you signed up to start school tomorrow, Phoebe. Wouldn't that be great?"

"Deal," said Jack as he headed off toward the community center.

"I already got a school. Remember, Mom?"

Maggie got down on one of her knees, held Phoebe's hand, and looked her in the eyes. "I know, Phoebe. With Mrs. Hutchins. And all your friends. I know you love your school. But now we're going to be living here in Glasgow. Remember? And you get a new kindergarten. A new teacher. And new friends. How does that sound?"

"Okay, Mom."

Maggie gave Phoebe a deep, long hug and didn't let go until Phoebe started to squirm.

"Let's go, Mom. I want to see my new school."

To anyone else, this small, rather flat-looking building might've seemed a bit ordinary. But to Maggie, the door in front of her represented not so much a way in as a way out. There was nothing she wanted more than a new life for Phoebe, one with infinite doorways and possibilities.

As Maggie pulled open the heavy door, she was instantly struck by an unfamiliar and eerie sound—silence. She'd never been in a school that wasn't alive with the buzzing excitement of hundreds of children. She and Phoebe walked down the hall, listening to the echoing sound of each of their steps as they went. No one was around except a janitor at the far end of the hall, swishing a mop rhythmically from one side of the hall to the other. He must be listening to music on his headphones, Maggie assumed, because he hadn't looked up when the heavy front door slammed shut behind them.

"This way," whispered Maggie as she pointed to a small blue "office" sign with an arrow directing them to the right. The office door was open. Inside was a woman in her mid-thirties with short brown hair, black slacks, and a light blue sweater. Her back was to the door, as she tidied up a day's worth of chaos.

Maggie knocked softly on the open door. "Hello?" she asked.

"Yes, may I help you?" the woman said automatically as she turned around to face the door. Big brown eyes and a warm smile greeted them. She seemed to be relishing the little bit of quiet at the end of a long, loud day.

"Phoebe here would like to start kindergarten here tomorrow if that's possible."

"Possible?" The woman smiled at Phoebe. "We'd be delighted to have you join us. Just move?"

"Yes, we arrived today."

The woman opened one of the metal four-drawer file cabinets behind her and pulled out a rather tattered manilla folder. "Here you go. Just fill this out," she said as she handed the form and a pen to Maggie.

"Not sure about the address yet," stuttered Maggie.

"Just fill in what you know. We'll get the rest when you get settled. We'll need vaccine records, too." She turned to Maggie and then smiled at Phoebe. "I think you're really going to like Mrs. Franklin. My daughter had her for kindergarten a few years ago. She loved her!"

"I can write my name," offered Phoebe, as if this might be a crucial piece of information.

The lady handed Phoebe a pencil and a scrap piece of paper. Phoebe proudly took the pencil in her right hand and the paper in her left. And then she carefully formed each of the letters in her name. When Maggie passed her form back over, so too did Phoebe. The lady chuckled.

"You both did a very nice job! We are definitely excited that you'll be joining us tomorrow, Phoebe. My name is Mrs. Jansen. School starts promptly at eight o'clock. See you then, Phoebe."

A job for Maggie, and a new school for Phoebe. Not bad for just under two hours. *Next up? A place to live*, thought Maggie as the two of them headed down the hall and out the front door.

"Let's go find Jack," said Maggie as they made their way across the street to the community center.

Chapter Seventeen

Monday afternoon, 5 p.m.

The board at the community center was loaded with notices for part-time work. General maintenance, shoveling snow, painting, odd jobs, repairs. You name it, someone in Glasgow needed it done. *If I lived here*, thought Jack, *I'd do okay. I could make a nice living.* He was, after all, a jack-of-all-trades. He'd never found his niche, but he'd learned to be a pretty good handyman. He'd spent a decent amount of time in the hardware store back home—and a fair amount of time fixing things for his mum.

When he was seven, Jack had come home from school one day to find his mum under the kitchen sink with water spewing everywhere. She was crying. Water from the sink, water from her eyes, water everywhere. Jack didn't know what to do, so he started crying too.

"Mum, what's wrong?" he cried.

"It's broken. It's all broken. And I can't fix it," she sobbed.

"I'll go get help," Jack said as he stood up and headed to the hardware store. There was nothing he wanted more than to help his mum. It'd been a tough year for her, with his dad running off again. His dad was always running off. Even worse, he was always coming back. "We don't need him, Mum," Jack would mutter. But Jack knew that wasn't completely true. They needed something. His mom was working two jobs, and Jack was either trying to be everything—or nothing. Because when his dad was home, it was best if Jack wasn't.

Jack ran the whole way to the hardware store, and he didn't stop once until he reached the front door. Then he stopped, wiped the tears from his eyes with his shirt-sleeve, and walked in. Upon seeing the tear-streaked, panicked face of little Jack, the owner of the hardware store politely excused himself from his customer, walked over to Jack, and led him to the back.

"Okay, Jack, what's going on, buddy?"

"It's the sink, Hank. Water's shooting everywhere."

"Okay, which sink?"

"The one in the kitchen."

"Okay. Leaking under the sink?"

"Yeah."

"All right. Come with me, Jack. Let's go back to the faucet aisle. We'll find the right one, and I'll show you how to fix it."

The two of them walked together down the aisles for what would be the first of many times. By learning how to fix leaky faucets, broken washers, and clogged up lawnmowers, Jack started to discover how things work. Mechanical things, anyway. If he hadn't fixed something before, he could generally figure out how to do it. And he wasn't afraid to try. Yeah, Glasgow could work for him. It was as good a town as any, he figured. It was close enough to where he needed to go to clean things up with his past, yet still far enough away. Far enough away from anyone he didn't want to run into. Maybe when he got things cleaned up at home, he could come back and start over here.

And maybe, just maybe, he could help Maggie and Phoebe get settled and start over too. It felt good to be of help to someone. He wasn't sure how any of this was going to work, but he was willing to roll with it. For now anyway.

Chapter Eighteen

Monday afternoon, 5 p.m.

"Mom, there's Jack!" yelled Phoebe as she and Maggie entered the community center, which was basically one large room with four blank walls and a few rows of folding chairs stacked in the corner. Phoebe let go of Maggie's hand and ran across the empty space to hug Jack's leg as he stood in front of an old cork bulletin board.

"Hey, Jack," said Maggie.

"I'm going to school tomorrow, Jack," said Phoebe. "What are you doing?"

"Looking for stuff," Jack answered. He grinned at Maggie as he pointed to one flyer in particular.

"Apartment for rent," read Maggie. "Hey, it's even furnished. Will you go look at it with us Jack? It says just ask at the grocery store."

"Looks like the best one out there," he replied.

"Duh," said Maggie. "It's the only one." She playfully poked him in the ribs.

Within minutes, they were being escorted up the old wooden stairs at the back of the grocery store by an elderly man named Tom. The grocery store owner, assumed Maggie. "One block from the diner and just around the corner from the school," said Tom. "You can't beat the location." The living room was big enough, Maggie noted, furnished with an old, comfortable-looking sofa. And huge windows overlooking one of the town's little parks.

The kitchen was complete with all the dishes and plates they'd need, plus an old Formica kitchenette table from the fifties. "Quaint," whispered Jack. "Just like Mum's." Phoebe's little hand slipped unnoticed out of Maggie's. Down the hall she skipped to the door at the end. "Oh look, Mom. This bed is big enough for all three of us!" Maggie sheepishly followed Phoebe's trail of excitement down the hall, looked in, and saw an oversized four-poster bed. Jack chuckled at Maggie's instant unease.

"I'm not staying, Phoebe. This is for you and your mom."

"Mom, can't Jack stay with us? Please? Pretty please?"

"Jack's going to go see his mom, Phoebe. Remember? He's just here for a little while."

"Can't he have a sleepover, Mom? Please? Just this one time."

Maggie thought for a moment. One night. *What's the big deal?* she wondered. For some unknown reason, she trusted Jack.

"I think we're going to take this place. It's perfect," Maggie said to Tom. Then she turned to Jack. "You're welcome to stay here for the night, Jack." After a moment, she added, "You get the sofa, of course."

"Follow me downstairs, Ms. Maggie, and I'll get you to sign a little lease document. Then it's all yours." The four of them wandered back down the old wooden stairs and back into the grocery store. After signing, Maggie picked up the essentials: milk and cereal for the morning, a loaf of bread, a jar of peanut butter, and a pink sequined coin purse that Phoebe couldn't take her eyes off of. Then the three of them headed back up the stairs.

"Phoebe, you and me—this is our room," Maggie announced as she set her backpack on the bed. She pulled out Phoebe's toothbrush and Mr. Snuggles. "Jack, you get the living room. But right now, we've got some more work to do, Ms. Phoebe. Let's head back over to the diner to let Sally know I'm ready to start tomorrow."

"I'm going to go check on a few things myself," said Jack as he grabbed his jacket and followed the two of them out the door and down the stairs. "See you back here in a bit," he added before he headed across the park.

As Maggie and Phoebe walked through the door of the diner, it was obvious it was close to dinner time. There were customers at the counter and all the tables were taken. *We'll make this quick*, thought Maggie. *Sally's got her hands full at the moment.*

"Well, hello, ladies!" called Sally as she loaded up her tray with beverages. "I was hoping we'd see you again!"

"Hi, Sally. You the only one working here?" asked Maggie.

"Pretty much. Just me and Brandon the cook. He's in charge of the kitchen. I'm in charge of the floor. See why we need you so badly?"

"I get it. Well, Phoebe's all set for school, we found a place to live, and we're all settled in. I can start in the morning."

"That'd be awesome, Maggie. You'll have the nine to two shift. That'll work with Phoebe's schedule. But since tomorrow's your first day, can you make it a little early? Eight o'clock? So I can show you around before we get too busy. And I'll get you out of here by one-thirty. How's that?"

"Eight o'clock it is! I'll see you then," said Maggie as she and Phoebe headed back out the door.

"Fresh starts for both of us, young lady," said Maggie as she squeezed Phoebe's hand tightly. "I don't know about you, but I'm excited for tomorrow."

"Me too, Mom. Kindergarten! My first day at my second kindergarten!"

"What do you say we pick up some KFC on our way home? We have plenty of reason to celebrate," said Maggie.

Everything in this town was just a stone's throw away, as they say. From school to the diner to KFC, and in no time at all, they were heading back up the stairs to their new place.

"Jack?" called Maggie as they entered the apartment. "You here?" She was hoping he would be there. They hadn't locked the door. He could've just come back and settled in.

No answer.

Maggie pulled two dishes out of the cabinets, placed them on the table, and filled the plates with chicken and mashed potatoes. "What do you say? Should we set some aside for Jack?" asked Maggie.

"Where is Jack, Mom?"

"I thought he'd be back by now. Not really sure where he is, honey. But let's eat. You've got a big day tomorrow!"

Maggie and Phoebe sat down to what would be the first meal in their new home. It wasn't fancy. Neither the apartment nor the meal. But everything seemed just right. A chicken leg, a scoop of mashed potatoes, and a dab of gravy. Perfect, actually. Just as they were finishing, Jack knocked at the door. Maggie didn't ask where he'd been, and he didn't offer. "We saved you some dinner, Jack. I wasn't sure if you'd be hungry or not."

"Always hungry," was his answer as he filled his plate, sat down, and started to eat.

"I'm starting at the diner tomorrow," Maggie told him. "I've got the nine to two shift, but Sally wants me to start early my first day. Eight o'clock."

"And I'm starting school!" shouted Phoebe.

"Great news, guys," Jack replied.

"Will you walk me to school tomorrow, Jack? Please?" asked Phoebe.

"I would be honored to," said Jack. "And when I come back from Mum's, we'll get an orange soda." He winked at Phoebe and then looked nervously at Maggie, as if to check himself.

Maggie smiled. *So, Jack is coming back*, she thought. And what a relief that he offered to take Phoebe to school tomorrow. Maggie hadn't quite figured out how she was going to handle that.

"I didn't get to meet my teacher today," Phoebe explained as Jack busily consumed his mashed potatoes, "but the lady at my new school was the nicest one there."

"I bet the kids are great, too," added Jack. "I was trying to remember how old I was when we lived here. I was pretty little. I don't remember much. But my mum will. I'll ask her when I see her. She remembers all that stuff."

"Mine too," said Phoebe. "School starts at eight o'clock, right, Mom?"

"Yep, that's right, young lady. And now it's time for you to get ready for bed. A real bed," said Maggie. "Come on, Phoebe; say good night to Jack and follow me."

"Good night, Jack," sang Phoebe as she skipped down the hall behind her mother.

After a quick bath and a short bedtime story, Phoebe was all tucked into bed for the night.

"Good night again, Jack," Phoebe called softly from the bedroom. "Don't let the bedbugs bite."

"Good night, Phoebe," came the masculine response. "Good night, Maggie."

An hour or two before dawn, Phoebe whined a bit and snuggled in tighter to Maggie, seeking warmth from the early morning chill. "I'll get another blanket, sweetie," Maggie whispered. She rose from the bed, covered herself with a throw, and grabbed two more blankets from the bedroom closet. *I gotta remember to get us some pajamas tomorrow*, she thought. She laid the blanket over Phoebe and patted her on the back. Quietly, she carried the second blanket to the living room and stood over the sofa, watching Jack as he slept. His long, lean body stretched beyond the sofa's end. A naked leg had escaped the confines of the blanket and was dangling off the side. A lean, muscular leg. Maggie's eyes moved from the leg up to his torso and then slowly to his face. A strikingly beautiful face, with chiseled features softened by a youthful playfulness. She lingered there a moment, as she studied him. Unnoticed. She draped the blanket slowly, lovingly over his body. Without thinking, she bent down and brushed her lips against his. Startled by her actions, she stood up quickly and retreated to the safety of her bedroom.

Chapter Nineteen

Tuesday morning, 7 a.m.

As Jack woke and rubbed his eyes, he wondered, *Did I just dream about Maggie?* He sat up, a bit puzzled, and pulled on his jeans. Just then, he heard little noises coming from the bedroom. "I'm hungry, Mom," the familiar refrain trickled down the hall. Jack laughed. He admitted it was a bit strange to be here, staying in someone else's little world, but it was a lot better than where he'd been living for the past four years.

"I appreciate the hospitality, ladies. I'll be heading out to see my mum this morning," Jack said at breakfast as he shoveled in another mouthful of Coco Puffs. Phoebe looked up, surprised.

"Will you walk me to school today? Like you promised?"

"Planning on it, Phoebe," Jack replied as he wiped the chocolate milk from the corners of his mouth. "My train leaves precisely twenty minutes after your first school bell rings." He held up the train schedule he'd stuffed in his pocket the other day. "So you first and then me."

Maggie poured herself another cup of coffee and then slithered into her chair across from Phoebe. *I need a second cup*, she thought. *Today will be a big day.* "I'm working the day shift," she reminded Phoebe, "so I can meet you after school."

"Is there really a bell for school?" queried Phoebe, after thinking about Jack's last comment.

"I guess we'll find out, young lady." Jack chuckled as he excused himself from the table. "If you ladies don't mind, I might borrow your shower before heading out to see my mum."

Maggie cleared the dishes, stacked them neatly in the sink after dumping all the stray Cocoa Puffs into the garbage can, and let the water run over the top of them for a minute. Phoebe handed Maggie her old pink comb and smiled. "A pony please, Mom." Maggie dried her hands on the bright yellow dish towel and turned toward Phoebe. She brushed Phoebe's hair with long, even strokes, collecting every stray strand she could find. Once she had them all collected, she wound the band carefully around them, restoring order to what had been a mess just moments before.

"Go put your dress on, and you're ready for the day, Phoebe."

Moments later, Jack and Phoebe were standing at the front door, waiting for Maggie's final inspection. "There's a peanut butter sandwich in your backpack, Phoebe. And a new pencil." She turned to Jack. "I packed you a sandwich as well, Jack."

Jack nodded in appreciation. He gave Maggie a quick, awkward hug. He was going to miss these two, he realized as he put his sandwich in his coat pocket. He smiled sadly. *How ironic*, he thought. *Here I am, feeling responsible for these two. Like I've never felt for anyone before.* Then he could almost hear his mother: "Better clean up one mess before you start a new one." Jack nodded to himself as he shut the door behind him and Phoebe.

Once on board the train, Jack pulled out an old worn sheet of paper. He unfolded it carefully and set it down in front of him, looking backward to make sure no one was reading over his shoulder. *Does it even matter?* he wondered. Old coffee stains dotted the page. The edges had been worn thin where his fingers had rubbed them mindlessly. And the folds were about to give way. Many hours of deep, honest reflection had gone into this page. "Mom," it began. What followed were probably the only honest words Jack had ever written. As he sat back and looked at the page, he could almost hear the sage advice he had received while behind bars: "Own your part. Don't talk about hers. This is your apology, Jack, not hers." What would her part have been anyway? Allowing Jack to be Jack. Not wanting him to hurt, and ultimately, hurting him deeply because of it. And his? Again, his mind started to wander through the once familiar streets of his childhood. Before he knew it, Jack was sound asleep, rocking along on the train with dozens of strangers, each going somewhere.

"Wolf Point. Next station Wolf Point, Montana!" bellowed the conductor as she sashayed her way down the train car, collecting ticket stubs. Jack woke quickly, rubbed his eyes, and stared out at the all-too-familiar, quickly-approaching station. It hadn't changed a bit. The old simple structure with its classic gabled roof, blue walls, and white trim still had garbage cans on the platform out front, bulging with crushed soda cans, candy wrappers, and crumpled brown paper bags. *Maybe it's the same trash*, thought Jack, silently chuckling. But as he stepped off the train, duffle bag flung over his shoulder, he noticed a lot of activity, a lot of energy that really didn't belong to the quiet little town of Wolf Point. That's when he saw the flashing lights, a police car, and the town's entire fleet of cops—all three of them. Jack didn't like the looks of this at all. "They're certainly not here for me, not this time," Jack reassured himself as he jumped off the side of the platform and bolted toward Front Street.

Without even thinking about it, Jack made his way toward Chad's house. Of course, Chad wasn't there anymore. Chad wasn't anywhere. Rebecca might be, though. Not that she'd be eager to see him. *I'll make my way home*, he thought as he started to cut through Chad's yard. From Chad's house to Jack's, there was sure to be a path along the fence where the grass had long ago given up ever trying to grow. He could find his way home blindfolded. Lord knows he probably did once or twice, stumbling along the ground, throwing up along the way.

Commotion here as well, thought Jack as he caught sight of Chad's house. *Another cop car. What the hell?* He almost started to jog home, to his mom. No one had noticed him. He was sure of it. And he didn't feel like knocking on the door and asking questions. Not at Chad's house. Not at Rebecca's. Facing her the other day had been hard enough. He certainly didn't want to run into her again. Or worse, her parents.

As Jack approached his yard, he found his mom standing just inside the front door, staring out blankly. Slowing his pace, he stopped at the fence and softly called out her name. His name for her. "Mum." An older woman, worn about the edges and eons away in thought, she looked up slowly, absently.

"Jack." Her mouth formed the word behind the glass. It was as if she'd been waiting for him for a lifetime. He took this as an invitation, so he slowly opened the gate and walked toward the porch.

"Hi, Mum," he said as if to complete his sentence. She opened the front door and stepped out onto the front porch, and after another long pause, she reached out and pulled him into her. A long, deep hug. *None of this could have been easy for her*, he thought sadly. *Even before I arrived. She's had one hell of a hard life.*

Chapter Twenty

When Jack's mother finally spoke, she said none of the things she'd considered saying when she first saw her son again. None of the rehearsed lines or thoughts she'd carried with her all these years. It wasn't even about him. Or her.

"Did you come for Rebecca?" Ida asked.

"Rebecca? No, I came to see you, Mum."

"Rebecca's dead," she replied almost matter-of-factly.

Jack immediately sat down on the top step next to where his mom had been sitting. He couldn't even think of a question to ask. He just sat there. Rebecca? He had just seen Rebecca.

"What?" he asked.

"Yes, dead. I thought you'd heard. We don't know nothing yet. She came home to watch the cat. Her folks left for Glendive Monday night. And she was murdered this morning. Just hours ago. Their neighbor, Mrs. Blanchard, was out walking her dog and saw the front door wide open. She went inside and found Rebecca dead, shot. There was blood all over the place. It makes no sense at all." She sat down gently right beside him.

Jack didn't say a word. He just softly took hold of his mom's hand and held it.

"I was just making one of my casseroles to take over," she sputtered as she stood up. "I made two. Let me fix you a helping, Jack. You look hungry."

Jack couldn't eat. "I think I better head over to Rebecca's, Mum. You wanna join me?" he asked as he stood.

His mum shook her head. "No."

"I ran into her the other day, Mum. It was just yesterday. On the train," Jack said. "Thought I'd let Sam know. And maybe he knows what happened." He kissed her on her cheek like he'd always done as a child and started to head for the door.

"Give them my love, Jack, will ya? And this casserole." She followed him out the door, carrying the casserole pan. "I'm sure they won't be there yet. They're heading back from Glendive. But Sam will be. He'll make sure they get it."

Within minutes, Jack was one of the half-dozen neighbors wandering around the street outside of Rebecca's parents' house, hunting for answers, carrying a casserole dish.

"Someone entered Rebecca's house earlier this morning, shot her, and left. That's all we know at this point," Sam told the crowd. Sam had been the town's sheriff for forty years, and he'd never seen anything like this. *No one here has. Nothing like this*, thought Jack.

This would be the story that would outlive everyone here today—and their children and their children's children.

It will take a while for this to sink in, thought Jack, *for the town to absorb it. But right now, there's nothing to be done or learned here. Nothing I can do, so I'll do what I've come here to do.* Next right indicated thing, he reminded himself. He set the casserole dish on the porch next to a half-dozen other casserole dishes and headed for home.

As he rounded the corner, he saw his mum, sitting on the porch draped in a fuzzy blanket. She was right where he'd left her, waiting for him. "I'll take you up on that casserole now, Mum," he called out. "They don't know anything yet."

The two of them walked inside, with Jack just steps behind, following like a little puppy. The kitchen was filled with familiar smells from his youth: fresh coffee percolating, cinnamon and orange peels brewing on the stovetop, and tuna casserole just out of the oven. *Home*, thought Jack. *No matter where we go or what we do, we always find our way home.*

Ida scooped out an oversized portion of casserole and plopped it on a plate. (There'd be an extra pan, Jack knew, and his mom would freeze small servings wrapped in plastic wrap for her dinners this coming week and next.) She set the old china plate in front of Jack as she motioned for him to sit. "We're using the good stuff," she said, like she always said, as if this were a new idea. "Because what are we waiting for? Christmas?" Fine with Jack. But the funny thing was, the good stuff wasn't so good anymore. Chipped and faded, worn with use, kind of like his mother.

They sat together, facing each other at the table. She didn't say a word. It was now his turn.

"I'm sorry, Mum." There. He'd begun. Taking a deep breath, he continued. "I know. I'm sorry. I'm sorry. I'm sorry. It's all I ever say," said Jack. "Four years away did me some good, though. And I honestly am sorry. For all of it."

His mom looked deeply into his eyes, wondering if he really meant it this time. In the past, he'd say, "Mum, it wasn't my fault." Or another favorite line, "I didn't mean it, Mum." But it always started with "I'm sorry." At the end of the day, though, none of it changed his behavior or the way Ida really felt about her son. A mother's love just is. For some reason, it has nothing to do with what he did or didn't do, said or didn't say. It just is. One of the few things in this world that is completely unconditional, Ida figured. At least in her case.

"We'll see, Jack. Hopefully," was her response. Another truism in her world—no matter how small, some little speck of hope could always be found.

"I haven't been the son I could've been," Jack said. She nodded.

And then something happened, something she hadn't experienced in so long that she'd forgotten all about the emotions that surrounded it. He started crying. First a sputter, then a quiet gasp, and then sobs. Her five-year-old Jack had returned. She held him as she had when he was just a small boy and rubbed his back in circular motions, as if to help the sadness find its way out. Round and round she rubbed, quietly shushing and soothing the anguish of this overgrown child. Jack closed his eyes and sank into his mom. The sobs slowly subsided.

After a good five minutes, Jack stood up and stretched his hands out far to his sides. Ida stood as well and brushed down the creases in her now wrinkled skirt. They looked deeply into each other's eyes and smiled timidly. "Okay," was the one thought that came to Ida's mind. "Okay." At that moment, the two of them returned to their tasks at hand, as if nothing had happened. Ida tucked the lone loose gray strand of hair behind her ear and started to put away the tuna casserole; Jack wiped his eyes and then wiped down the table, starting in one corner and methodically wiping from one side to the other, clearing away every single crumb, every smudge. The cleaner the table became, the more he scrubbed. By the time he put the washcloth away, the table looked brand new. Jack smiled.

From the kitchen sink, Ida watched her son as he stood back and inspected the sparkling clean table. He'd been such a tender boy, she reflected, almost too soft for this world. "I'm going to make him tougher," Jack's father had muttered when he went after Jack. He'd go after Jack, and Jack would just keep on going.

Most times when Jack would leave the house, he'd go to Chad's. He'd stay there for a night or two, usually until his dad had forgotten what he was so mad about or that Jack wasn't "man" enough. His dad would cool off; Jack could be Jack; and Ida could enjoy a reprieve from what seemed like an endless, pointless ongoing feud. Even though he wasn't home, Ida knew Jack was in better hands when he was at Chad's. Unpredictable and violent, his dad's anger was frightening. She'd tried to reason with her husband. She'd tried to stand up to him. She'd tried to insert herself between his anger and her son. But that had just made things worse for Jack, and she knew it. There was nothing she could do, she had reasoned. Nothing. Except make sure that when Jack did come home, there'd be some hot food waiting for him. It wasn't much, but it was something and something was better than nothing, she had figured.

Of course, as Jack got older, he didn't just go to friends' houses. He might start there, but then he'd be off and running. And there was no bringing him home at that point. The few times he had ended up in jail for a stint or two, it was almost a relief to Ida. She could put her head on her pillow and know that he was safe. If nothing else, he was safe. And for the mother of a troubled child, that can be good enough. And good enough can be everything.

Chapter Twenty-One

Tuesday afternoon, 1:55 p.m.

An apple, two rice cakes with peanut butter smeared on top, and a little box of raisins. Phoebe's after-school snack was waiting for her on the kitchen table and Maggie was waiting for her by the door. Five minutes 'til two. *Almost time*, thought Maggie, as she slowly put on her coat. *Glad I got off early today. This*, thought Maggie, *this is how life should be*. And it was how she remembered her childhood— two small plates of cookies and two small glasses of milk. One for Maggie, and one for her mom. "Cheers," her mom would say as the two of them clinked their glasses together, tossed them back, and then placed them down on the counter. "And what was the best part of today?" her mom would ask. Maggie would've considered her answer the entire way home from school, mulling over each possible highlight before selecting just the right one. This, of course, was before the cancer, when her mom was still present and still her mom. Was that the moment when Maggie's life switched direction? Was it the cancer, she wondered, when her life veered off just a little to the left? She wasn't sure, but now was her time, her moment. She grabbed her keys, looked up at the clock, and headed out the door.

Good thing Phoebe's school is so close, thought Maggie, as she quickened her pace just a bit. "Phoebe!" she called from two houses down as she noticed Phoebe standing out front, looking in both directions. "Phoebe!" she yelled a bit louder as she waved her arms in both directions. Phoebe looked up, embarrassed.

"Hi, Mom," Phoebe mumbled. She bent down to pick up her backpack. "Where's Jack?" she asked as she looked just beyond her mother. "He promised me a pop after school."

"He went to see his mom today. Remember?"

"Oh, yeah," said Phoebe.

"A pop? When did you start drinking pop, Phoebe?" asked Maggie with feigned disgust. "I have something better for you. Come with me." Maggie gently reached down and took hold of Phoebe's tiny hand. "Want me to carry your backpack, honey?"

"No, Mom. I got it. Orange pop, Mom. Jack says it's really good."

As they climbed the long narrow stairs to their new home, Phoebe asked, "Will Jack come back?"

Maggie smiled. "I certainly hope he comes back, Phoebe."

"Will he bring his mom?"

"I don't think he's bringing his mom back with him. But maybe we can meet her one day," said Maggie. *Who knows?* wondered Maggie. She smiled at the thought of Jack sticking around for a while.

As mother and daughter entered the apartment, Phoebe dropped her backpack on the floor, creating a loud thud. "Two! One for me and one for you!" shouted Phoebe. "Come on, Mom. Come sit down. I'll share my raisins with you!" she added as she slipped off her jacket and tossed it on top of her backpack. Clearly, this was much better than orange pop, Maggie thought proudly to herself. Yep, much better than orange pop—any day.

Maggie realized there's was no way for her to contact Jack again even if she wanted to because he had no cell phone. And she didn't either. She'd given hers away to that stranger on the train. It was just her and Phoebe, which was rather nice. This was their time to establish new routines, to create a new normal. Maggie's hope was to establish some sense of structure and create a sense of calm. Phoebe's world had lacked both up to this point. There had been some rough patches, for sure. Maggie believed she had shielded Phoebe from a lot of what was happening, but children know more than they're ever given credit for. Their environment seeps into their cells and alters their DNA. For the most part, Matt had adored Phoebe. The first year of her life, he'd spend the first hour of each day gently rocking her. But little things would set him off, and initially, he blamed Maggie for everything. "Can you make her stop crying?" he'd scream. "Don't you know anything?" Maggie's fear was that at some point he'd direct his anger toward Phoebe. But as long as he didn't, she was able to soldier on, as they say.

Chapter Twenty-Two

Tuesday afternoon, 2:15 p.m.

Becca Becca Rebecca. Murdered. A quiet, eerie stillness had drifted over the town, much like a heavy afternoon fog. No one seemed to be saying much. There wasn't much to say. But everyone seemed to be watching everyone else a little more closely. As Ida shuffled into the market, basket in hand, she, too, seemed to be scrutinizing her neighbors. Frank from across the street had always complained a bit about Rebecca's family, thought Ida. And didn't that old biddy two streets over hold a grudge against Rebecca's mom? Ida couldn't quite remember the details, but obviously it hadn't been anything that should've ended in murder. Maybe Rebecca owed someone money? Lots of money. Perhaps an old, unsettled debt?

As Ida wandered down the aisles, she pretended to be studying the produce as she typically did on Tuesday mornings. But on this particular Tuesday, she found herself following a little more closely behind the other shoppers, hoping to hear more, learn more, about what happened. "Must've been a jealous boyfriend," someone speculated. "Hadn't Rebecca just returned to town a few days ago?" "A drug deal gone bad?"

One woman in her early thirties and pushing a cart with two toddlers in it was talking to an older woman, possibly her mother. The older woman kept reaching over, trying to get the little girl to sit down. The girl would have none of it, bouncing up and down, poking at her little brother who was on the verge of tears. The younger woman shook her head. "So tragic for Rebecca's parents!" she exclaimed. "Haven't they suffered enough?" Taking her eyes off the bouncing toddler, Ida nodded to herself, as if the woman had been talking to her. Yes, they've been through enough. Lost both children, Ida considered as she blushed, feeling partly responsible for outcomes beyond her control.

Just then, Jack stepped up beside her and started to toss some items into her basket. "I'll make dinner tonight, Mum. My specialty." He took the basket from her, loading it up as they went down the aisle. Two cans of Hunt's tomato paste. A bag of elbow pasta. One can of black beans. Ida mindlessly watched as Jack took over. "After this, I'm heading to Hank's hardware to pick up stuff to fix that broken faucet of yours. Want to join me, Mum?" Ida shook her head. She'd rather be home. Felt safer there. Jack pulled out his old, tattered wallet, paid for the groceries with his last twenty, helped the clerk bag them, and then carried them to Ida's old blue Datsun. "Leave them in the trunk, Mum. I'll bring them in when I get home." He held her elbow as she lowered her body slowly into the car, then patted the door twice after he closed it. "I'll be home soon," he said and off he headed down the street to Hank's.

Chapter Twenty-Three

Tuesday afternoon, 2:45 p.m.

Jack's long, lanky legs covered a lot of ground without a lot of effort. By appearances, he seemed to take the entire world in stride. Which was exactly the opposite of how he felt. Jack couldn't stop thinking about his encounter with Rebecca the other day. Freaky timing, really. What the hell had happened? Aside from her surprise in running into him unexpectedly, nothing had seemed to be wrong with Rebecca. She didn't seem unnecessarily worried or hurried about anything. As Jack rounded the corner, he saw a cluster of folks gathered outside of Hank's. Yep, this might be where to go if you have a broken faucet to fix. But if you want to know something, anything, about what's going on in town, this was definitely the place to be.

"A neighbor found her. On the floor. Blood everywhere."

"Oh God, her poor parents."

"Haven't they been through enough?"

"But what happened?"

"Gunshot wound to the head. Close range. Or maybe a shotgun."

"I heard it was a baseball bat."

"No idea who did this?"

"Was anything stolen? Did they break in? Was she assaulted?"

"One gunshot wound to the head," Sam stepped in to clarify. "She died instantly. There weren't no struggle. Nothing seems to be missing. Motive unknown." Waving his arms in a sweeping motion, Sam added, "That's all we know, folks. Now move along. We'll let you know what we know when we know it." Jack was at the back of the crowd, listening intently. "Jack. Is that you, Jack?" Sam called. As sheriff, Sam knew everyone, everyone's business, and then some. "How the hell are you?" Sam took a few steps forward, grabbed Jack by the shoulders, and pulled him in for a tight embrace. "How the hell are you, buddy?"

"I'm doing good, Sam. Doing good. Just came up to visit Mum for a bit. She's doing pretty good, too."

"I guess you heard about Rebecca. Damn shame." Sam shook his head and scratched his graying beard. "Hey, Cindy would want to have you guys up for supper tonight." Sam's face brightened. "Cindy'd love to see ya. You and Ida. You were always one of her favorites."

"That'd be real nice, Sam. Mum would like that too. She'd like that a lot better than my cooking, I'm sure."

"Okay. I'll give you guys a call later. I'd better get back to it. We got some serious work to do here. Got to find our killer," said Sam, as he slowly rubbed the top of his head, deep in thought.

Jack started to head up the street, but then he remembered he'd forgotten what he had come for—a new faucet. One quick rotation of his right leg and he was headed back into Hank's. It wasn't so crowded now. Most people had gone on their way, having gotten what they'd come for. It was still so astonishing that Rebecca had been murdered. He hadn't heard anything about her parents. They must be back from Glendive by now. Jack pictured all their neighbors, working together, bringing baskets of food to them, wherever they might be staying. Maybe at a neighbor's house? He wasn't sure. He couldn't imagine what they were going through. Not this time. They'd been through this before, just four years ago. Jack tried to focus on hardware to keep from thinking those dark thoughts that had been keeping him awake all these years. Faucets. Aisle 4. Back left corner. He knew this. But who could've done this to Rebecca? That's something Jack couldn't even begin to imagine.

Chapter Twenty-Four

Tuesday afternoon, 4:15 p.m.

Ida didn't get out much these days. Grocery store on Tuesdays. Church on Sundays. That was about it. A Tuesday evening at Cindy and Sam's—that would be a welcomed treat. She'd insisted on bringing something, maybe her banana pudding with vanilla wafers on top? But Cindy wouldn't have any of it. "Just you, Ida. Just you and Jack." Ida took special care in finding something to wear. She went through her entire closet and ended up with what she had worn to the store yesterday. Her favorite, a blue dress with small white polka dots, and that's all that mattered. "It's not so much the clothes but how they make you feel," she always said. She had carefully washed her hair that morning so it would look its best. Pinned it back on the left side with her favorite tortoise shell comb, just behind her ear. Even put on a dab of lipstick, something reserved for special occasions.

"You almost ready, Jack? They're expecting us at four-thirty," her small voice called from the bedroom.

Jack glanced in the mirror. He licked the palm of his hand and then slicked down his hair where it had been standing up and grinned widely to check his teeth and gums for leftover lunch— "Yep, Mum. All set." He grabbed his coat, sauntered out of the room, and met her at her bedroom door. "Let's go, Mum." He held the door for her, and then the two of them headed up the back hill to where her blue Datsun stood ready. Protected not by a garage, but merely by an old carport, the blue Datsun remained sheltered from some of the elements some of the time. Not so in the winter, though, when the winds were fierce and the snows piled high. Jack turned and looked at his mother, going at her own pace, a slow pace, and yet she always managed to get where she was going, never even so much as a minute late.

It was just a few minutes' ride to Cindy and Sam's. Ida always insisted on driving. At the speed of Ida. *I could walk and get there faster*, thought Jack, grinning as he looked out the passenger side window, noting how nothing had changed in the four years he had been gone. No new paint on any of the houses. No freshly planted trees. No new cars in any driveways. The only thing different here— Chad was gone. And now Rebecca.

When they pulled up in front of the small bungalow-style house, Sam was waiting for them, sitting on the front porch in an old rocking chair, shaded by a large frost-covered elm. Soft country music was coming from inside the house.

"So good to see you, Ida. I'm glad you two could come. Cindy loves to cook, you know. And she always makes more than the two of us can eat." Sam stood as he led them into the house. The smell of lasagna and freshly baked chocolate chip cookies greeted them as they stepped inside. Cindy took off her apron and offered them seats in the front room. Jack looked around. Nothing had changed in this room either. Even the tiny figurine of the female skater on the mantel was as she had always been, pirouetting gracefully, effortlessly.

Everyone sat down. Sam across from Jack, next to Cindy. Ida on the far side, next to the mantle. No one said a word. The air didn't seem to move; it just hung there. Jack looked at his hands. Ida sat on the edge of her seat.

"This winter isn't going away all too fast, is it?" asked Sam. It was the kind of thing one says when one doesn't know what to say but something needs to be said. He scratched his head. No one moved. No one responded. Then Cindy leaned in, right past the awkwardness of the moment, and gently grabbed Jack's hand.

"Jack, we've missed you. Good to have you back with us."

"Yeah, Jack," added Sam.

"Horrible what happened," said Cindy. "To both Chad and to you, Jack." The room seemed to expel a collective breath. Even the light seemed to soften. Jack released a lungful of air.

And Ida let out the words she'd been storing for days. "I can't believe that Rebecca is dead."

A sense of energy replaced the room's stillness. Sam shook his head rapidly.

"We still don't know who did it. But we do have something," he whispered, as if letting these three in on confidential police business. Ida and Jack leaned in closer.

"We just don't know much yet," said Sam. "But we did find a cell phone by her body. We checked with her folks. They'd never seen it before. They don't think it's hers."

"I meant to tell ya, Sam. I saw her on the train yesterday," said Jack.

"Wonder where she was headed," said Sam. "Did you get the chance to talk to her?"

"She got on at Cut Bank. Off at Havre. No idea why she got off there. She didn't say. She might've gotten off just to get away from me," Jack replied.

Cindy reached out her hand and patted Jack's knee. "Don't say that, honey."

"Do you think the cellphone belongs to the killer?" asked Ida, shifting attention away from Jack.

"Why would she have two cell phones? Was she selling drugs?" asked Cindy, who had just finished watching an episode of her favorite crime show.

Sam shook his head slowly. "We're hoping there might be some prints on the phone."

Everyone got quiet for a moment.

To break the silence, Sam said, "We do know the phone is from Whitefish. It's got a Whitefish prefix or whatever you call it."

Whitefish? Odd, thought Jack. *Maggie and Phoebe's hometown.*

"Hard to imagine anyone here would do such a thing," blurted Ida. She'd had a bit of trouble sleeping last night. Checking twice to make sure all the doors were locked. Closing the curtains. She looked across the room at Jack and felt reassured; she liked having him home again.

"Well, Ida, don't worry. We'll get to the bottom of this." Sam crossed his arms confidentially.

Cindy stood. "Enough of this! I think it's time we eat." She headed to the dining room, beckoning everyone to follow. "Sit!" she commanded as she went into the kitchen to retrieve the feast. As the three took their places at the table, Jack realized how hungry he was. A large bowl of fresh salad, a perfectly buttered and toasted loaf of garlic bread, and a huge pan of homemade lasagna. Nothing else seemed to matter at the moment. Jack was in heaven. The conversation lightened. And before long, Jack and Ida were on their way home, with full bellies and light hearts.

Chapter Twenty-Five

Tuesday afternoon, 4:15 p.m.

Nailed it, thought Maggie. The rice cakes smeared with peanut butter—that was always her favorite too. *Mom would be proud*, Maggie imagined. Okay, maybe not proud. Maybe a bit horrified with all that had happened recently. But for this particular moment, for this tiny victory, her mom would be proud. Maggie was sure of that.

These past twenty years, there had been dozens of times when Maggie would imagine that her mom was proud. Or disappointed. Or pleased. *Oh, Mom's angry now*, she'd scold herself quietly. Or, *I can almost hear her laughing at that.* By imagining how her mom might respond, Maggie managed to keep her mom alive and with her.

Maggie had been only a couple of years older than Phoebe was now when she lost her mom to cancer. "Lost" as they say. As if cancer came in and quietly removed her. She was there, and then lost, gone forever. No, that's not how it was. No, cancer came in and slowly ate away at the woman who had brought Maggie into the world. It stole her strength. Slowly. It chewed away at her energy. Relentlessly. It distracted her. It gnawed away at her resolve. Her focus. And finally, it took all there was except for her love for Maggie and her husband. And then she was gone.

As Maggie's mom faded away, so too did her dad. He'd go to the garage, his shop, and he'd tend to things that needed tending to. A broken lamp. A flat tire on a bike no one ever rode. A clogged motor on a rusty old lawn mower. If it was broken, he'd spend endless hours trying to fix it. Because the one thing he wanted to fix he couldn't.

A thirty-seven-year-old man and a seven-year-old girl, struggling to stay afloat in a world that was falling apart. That's how Maggie remembered that last year and a half of her mom's life.

Maggie looked over at Phoebe. There was now a trail of peanut butter smeared from the corner of her mouth all the way to her nose. *I wanted you to have two loving, supportive parents*, thought Maggie as she looked at Phoebe. *I wanted your young life to be without strife or sorrow. Just love.* To date, that's not what Phoebe had experienced, Maggie admitted. *No, but things can change. They will. They have to.*

It had started out as a perfect marriage. She'd found the guy who was everything she'd dreamt of. Attentive, loving, protective. She finally had a home that was hers—where she felt like she belonged. She had a place on this earth and a man who loved her. But the man she married was not the same man as the one she was married to now. That man seemed always on edge, filled with anger and blame. "Why is this house a mess? It's always a mess. What do you do all day? Can't you dress a little nicer? Don't you have any pride in yourself?"

Nothing was ever good enough. Ever.

What had happened? What went wrong? Maggie would ask herself this question so many times.

Maybe Matt was right. Maybe she did ask for too much. Maybe it was all her fault. Maybe if she'd been a little less demanding—or a little more demanding—maybe everything would've turned out differently. By the time things had started to fall apart, Maggie didn't know what to do. She had no one to confide in, either. No close friends. Her family was gone. It was just the two of them. And then Phoebe.

Phoebe will make everything better, Maggie had told herself. *She will soften him.* But her arrival was followed by more yelling, and more blaming. "Why is she crying?" he'd rage. "Can't you make her stop? What's wrong with you?"

Maggie's head hurt.

This might've gone on for years. But one morning, as the snow was gently falling on the trees outside, Matt turned his head and directed his gaze toward Phoebe.

"Daddy, I don't wanna," Phoebe's little voice whined at the prospect of picking up her toys before naptime.

"You what?" asked Matt as he picked up Phoebe by the arms.

"I don't wanna," she whispered, knowing this wasn't the right answer at the time.

"You don't wanna? You don't wanna? Well, there are a lot of things I don't wanna. But I do them. I do them all day long!" he screamed.

Maggie was standing in the kitchen, unloading the dishwasher, nervously listening to this exchange. Instinctively, as Matt's voice rose, so too did the dish she was holding in her hands. She raised it a foot above her head and let it drop to the ceramic tile floor. It shattered into a thousand tiny pieces. In an instant, Matt's attention and all of his pent-up anger switched from Phoebe to Maggie. He released Phoebe, who quickly started to pick up each of her toys and place them in the toy box in the corner of the room. "What the hell is wrong with you?" he screamed, spraying his saliva all over Maggie's face. Closer and closer he stood, until he was just inches away, crowding her, suffocating her without even touching her. "Why are you so stupid?" he spewed. She stood there, with no place to go. She stood and she took every ounce of his anger and absorbed it. *I can do this*, she told herself. *I can be a buffer. I can protect her from him.*

And Maggie did take it. She took it. And she stored every little last bit of it deep inside her cells. Until one day, she couldn't take any more.

▞▞▞▞▞▞▞▞▞▞

"IF SHE DOESN'T STOP!" he had raged. *I know that look*, thought Maggie, as she swooped Phoebe up and ran into the barn, clutching her daughter tightly to her chest. *I can bar the door. I can keep him out.* She ran faster. Yet with each step she took, he took two.

He grabbed her sweater and pulled her back. She slipped from the sweater, rushed through the door, and slammed it shut. Not fast enough, though. He pushed it open before she had the chance to bolt it. With one shove, she fell to the hard, gravel ground, slicing her arm on an old rusty pitchfork that happened to lay there. Phoebe sobbed. "Run, Phoebe. Run!" Phoebe obeyed. With a bewildered look on his face, Matt turned to watch Phoebe tuck herself into the far corner of the barn, shielding her face from what was happening all around her. From the ground, Maggie grabbed hold of an old rusty shovel. She stood. Whack. And Matt went down. Hard. He did not come back up.

Quickly, Maggie ran to Phoebe, scooped her up, and fled from the barn. Outside, she stopped. Leaving her home frightened her— but what choice did she have? Behind her, an unconscious Matt was bleeding on the barn's hard gravel floor. A terrified Phoebe was in her arms. And blood, thick red blood was on her shirt. Maggie entered the house and grabbed her coat, her bag, Phoebe's little bag of books, and a change of clothes for Phoebe. And they were gone.

Looking back, Maggie realized how simple it all seemed now, after the fact. You make a decision. You take an action. And just like that, just like that switch on a train track, the trajectory of your life changes forever.

Chapter Twenty-Six

Tuesday morning, 7 a.m.

Once a hunter, always a hunter. "It's in our blood," Matt recalled hearing his grandfather say every October, at the beginning of their annual hunting trip. As a young boy, he had felt the excitement start to fill the house, weeks before, growing in intensity each day. His father would bring their special hunting rifles out of the gun safe and meticulously clean them, rubbing them almost sensually with oil, massaging them slowly, over and over. They would pack and repack their bags, carefully folding each pair of camouflaged pants, each thermal shirt, every pair of boxers. They would spend days preparing their food; filling their water bottles; stocking their canned goods, utensils, paper towels—fitting it all neatly into their backpacks. If they couldn't carry it, they couldn't take it. That was the rule. And oddly enough, it didn't even matter so much if they came home empty-handed. The thrill was in the hunt, in the pursuit.

Matt felt that excitement now, as a grown man, just a matter of miles from his prey. The moment Maggie had left on Monday morning, he'd turned on the remote tracking feature he'd installed in her phone. He packed his small camo duffle bag with every-thing he'd need, and nothing more. Two pairs of jeans, four pairs of black socks, four pairs of boxers, and four neatly folded long sleeve T-shirts. A toothbrush. Small tube of toothpaste. And his gun. He turned down the baseboard heat to save on energy. And he headed out the door.

He was glad he'd gotten her that cell phone last year. She hadn't really wanted one, had actually protested a bit. But he assured her it was for her own safety. "Anything could happen," he had told her. "Women get taken all the time." As her husband, he reasoned, it was his job to protect her. Yes, anything could happen. But he knew that's not what had happened this time. No, the pounding in his head told him otherwise. What had happened was clear. The question was: Why? He'd been a good husband. A faithful husband. And a loving father.

He held up his cell phone and reread the nine unanswered text messages he'd sent her in just the last few hours. All of which had been delivered. None of which had been answered. Yet. *Not yet*, he told himself as he settled into his car and started the engine.

He had taken his time, slept in an old motel along the way. Careful not to leave tracks, he had paid in cash. He didn't talk to anyone. He just kept moving. On Tuesday morning, before the sun rose, he had reached his destination. He stopped at a diner on the outskirts of town, ordered a huge breakfast—with all his favorites. He wanted everything to be just right today. Today was his day. He was bringing his girls home. He hadn't really considered how he was going to convince them to come. Or if he'd even have to. Somehow, he just assumed they would. Up until now, Maggie had always done what he suggested. She was a good wife. But obviously something had gotten into her lately. Once they were back home, he'd have a good long talk with her. They'd get things settled. And everything would go back to normal.

The waitress at the diner this morning had been a bit too chatty for Matt. He'd ordered and was done with her. But, apparently, she wasn't done with him.

"Where ya headed this morning?" she asked, leaning on the back of the seat opposite him.

Why is it when you want a woman to talk to you, she won't? thought Matt. *But every other time….*

"Nowhere in particular," was his non-response response.

"Been on the road for a while?" she asked.

"Nope."

"You staying in Wolf Point for a stretch?"

"Nope."

"'Cause if you do," she went on, "there's a good place for supper on the other side of town. A nice little restaurant with real good meatloaf."

Matt looked up at her blankly. She didn't seemed to notice.

"And the best strawberry shortcake I've ever had!"

Frustrated, Matt stood up. "Where's the bathroom?" She pointed to the opposite side of the restaurant. He nodded and pushed past her.

When he was finished, Matt slowly stuck his head out of the bathroom door and observed. He checked his table—she wasn't there. All clear. He spotted her at the counter chatting with three truckers who had just come in. *Maybe that'll keep her busy for a while*, he thought as he picked up a newspaper on the way back to his table. It would serve as a clever decoy, just in case she reappeared. He opened it up and started to flip through the pages. *What happens in a town like Wolf Point?* he wondered. *And why was his wife here?* Didn't really matter, he reminded himself. He'd found her, and she didn't even know it. The element of surprise. He smiled proudly.

After savoring every bite, Matt wiped his mouth and stood up from the table. He picked up his check, read it carefully, and placed a twenty-dollar bill beside his now spotless plate. Without so much as a nod to anyone, he walked out the door and was on his way.

Just two blocks away now. He pulled over for a moment to quiet his nerves. *I'll call her*, he thought. *Let her know I'm on my way.*

No response. Matt felt anger churning in his gut. He could understand the lack of response with texting. She hated texting. But a call? For her not to answer his call was like a slap in his face.

One more chance, he thought. *I'll give her one more chance.* He hit redial. No answer. The anger in his gut started to rise.

Matt set down the phone and drove the final two blocks. He parked right outside of the house where she was. He called one last time. Nothing. Absolutely nothing. He felt the anger reaching his chest. He texted. "WHERE THE HELL ARE YOU?"

And finally, after how many days and hundreds of texts, she responded, "WHO IS THIS?"

Who is this? Who is this? His anger was now pressing in on his temples. Who is this?

"YOU KNOW DAMN WELL WHO THIS IS, BITCH!" But that wasn't enough for Matt. One more now: "WHAT THE HELL IS WRONG WITH YOU? ANSWER YOUR DAMN PHONE!"

And then her second and final text came: "FUCK YOU."

That was it. That was the last thing Matt remembered.

Chapter Twenty-Seven

Tuesday morning, 7:30 a.m.

Early Tuesday morning, the sun crept in through the white linen curtains in the front room. The only sound was the old radiator cranking out heat. And the smell of freshly brewed coffee made Rebecca smile. She had made it home on time last night, minutes before her parents took off for their annual trip to Glendive to visit her dad's two brothers. She'd offered to stay with Rufus while they were gone, which was the least she could do—considering that senile old cat had started out as her kitten so many years ago. Besides, there was something comforting about coming home, curling up with old Rufus, and waking up in the house she grew up in.

She hadn't slept as well as she'd hoped to, though. Running into Jack on the train yesterday had brought up a lot of unexpected emotions. She'd made a point of not sharing any of this with her parents. Not now. She didn't know why Jack was out early. But she didn't want the news of his early release to dampen her parents' moods. They had actually seemed happy for the first time in years.

Rebecca poured herself a cup of coffee and walked over to the sofa. *A quiet Tuesday morning, with nothing to do. I can finally finish that novel I've been carrying around for weeks,* she thought. She sipped her coffee and reached for her bag. *I can't even remember what novel I'm reading.* Hadn't she promised herself she'd read every day? No matter what? Well, today was the day. No one around but Rufus. And there was a big pot of coffee in the kitchen ready to keep her warm for hours.

She reached into her bag for her book and pulled out all kinds of junk. Candy wrappers, an old scarf, a blue ballpoint pen, mascara, a hairbrush with bristles threaded with long dirty blond strands of hair, and a tattered sports bra. She dumped the contents out onto the floor. There in the middle of it all was a cell phone. She stopped moving for a moment. She picked it up slowly and brought it up to her face to study it. She turned it on. It wasn't dead. It wasn't even locked. She scrolled down. All the texts seemed to be coming from one person. Someone named Matt. *This Matt,* she thought, *seems to be a very angry man.*

Just then, a new text came through:

WHERE THE HELL ARE YOU?

"Okay, I don't know who you are or who you are talking to, but you are obviously an asshole," Rebecca said directly to the cellphone.

She started to scroll back more, to see how far back these angry texts went. Dozens and dozens of them.

WHO DO YOU THINK YOU ARE? WHERE THE HELL ARE YOU? WHAT'S WRONG WITH YOU?

Text after text after text. All one sided too. There were no responses, not even one.

This could be entertaining, thought Rebecca, as she stood up and walked to the kitchen for another cup of coffee. She returned to the sofa and started to read all the previous texts. She could almost feel the sender getting angrier and angrier with each text he sent.

At a safe distance, on a comfortable sofa, coffee cup in hand, Rebecca found herself entranced with the deranged mind of the sender. *A good distraction*, she thought. More fascinating than any book or movie on TV.

A new text arrived:

WHERE THE HELL ARE YOU?

Wow, thought Rebecca. *This guy is on fire. Okay, I'll stoke the flames.*

WHO IS THIS? was the message she sent.

YOU KNOW DAMN WELL WHO THIS IS, BITCH.

Seconds later, the phone started to vibrate. *Not talking to you, asshole*, thought Rebecca as she slowly, leisurely took another sip of coffee.

ANSWER YOUR DAMN PHONE said the text message.

She could almost feel his blood pressure rising with each new text he sent. *You know*, she thought, *if this were my phone, I'd dump it too. And I'd dump this asshole.* Then she set the phone down again.

It rang again.

WHAT THE HELL IS WRONG WITH YOU? ANSWER YOUR DAMN PHONE.

Okay, that's enough, thought Rebecca. *Party's over*. Never one to walk away from confrontation, she picked the phone back up. She took another big sip of coffee and stared thoughtfully at the last message. She smiled. Then she sent her final message.

FUCK YOU.

How was she to know that he was tracking the phone, or that he was right outside her house? How could she have known what blackout anger looks like for a person consumed by it? She never would find out either. Because when he barged through her front door, she hardly had the chance to get a look at him before he shot her in the head.

Chapter Twenty-Eight

Tuesday evening, 7:30 p.m.

Being home now with Mum was so much different than it ever was before. In the past, Jack had always been sneaking in or out, always running from something. Now, he rather enjoyed just sitting in the kitchen with Mum.

While Jack was growing up, his mum wasn't there much. But three chocolate chip cookies would be. They'd be on a small plate waiting on the counter, as if greeting him each day after school. Jack would bite into the first cookie, grab a glass of milk from the refrigerator, and sit down at the Formica table. He'd toss his backpack on the chair beside him. "My day was okay," he'd say out loud, as if he were answering the cookie's unspoken question. "I did good. I learned a lot," he'd announce to the second cookie.

But the cookie knew. Jack would've found himself lost in class, as his teacher droned on and on about numbers too high or countries too far away to matter to him.

He'd try to focus. He'd try to stick it out for an entire day. And most days, he would. What else was there to do anyway? Some days, though, he'd cut class and wander around town. He'd go to the hardware store, or swipe a Coke from the drugstore. But at three-thirty, he'd go home for his cookies. They were waiting for him.

He'd spend an hour at home each afternoon before he'd be off again, usually just moments before his dad would show up. Home from work, heading to the bar—that stretch of time where anything other than an ice cold beer was going to be met with rage. Jack had learned early on to get the hell out of that man's way.

Most nights, Jack would roam the neighborhood. He'd hang out at Chad's house. Or wander downtown. Sometimes he'd just walk the streets for an hour or two. But no matter what he did, he'd make it back home, and be back in bed by eleven. That was his rule. Because that's when Mum got home from her second job. He didn't want her to worry. And that's when his dad would be passed out, dead to the world.

By the time Jack got to high school, though, his iron clad rule got a little soft around the edges. What once was eleven turned into midnight. Sometimes 1 a.m. A few times, he wouldn't be back by the time his mom left for her day job.

Now, though, here he was, in the kitchen, watching his mum bake a coffee cake for the morning. He had no desire to go drinking, and she had no reason to worry. It was a good deal.

"Cindy called just a bit ago. She thanked us for coming to dinner tonight. And said they found out who the cell phone belongs to; that's what Sam said. Just as he thought. Someone in Whitefish."

"So now what?" asked Jack.

"They've notified the police over there. I suspect they'll go talk to the guy who owns it. Ida nodded. "And maybe we'll find out what happened," she added.

The mention of Whitefish reminded Jack of Maggie. "Gotta make a call, Mum. Do you mind?"

"Help yourself, Jack. I got some dishes to wash anyway," she replied.

Everyone had a cell phone these days, even kids. Everyone, that is, except Jack. And Maggie. Jack hadn't thought of it before, but why didn't Maggie have a phone? He picked up his mom's old-fashioned wall phone and called information.

"Yeah, can I have the number for Grizzly Groceries in Glasgow? Sure, I can wait." He knew why he didn't have a cell phone: No need for one where he'd been these past four years. But Maggie? "Okay, thanks!" he said as he jotted down the number on a scrap piece of paper. He called it. "Hey, Tom. Yeah, it's me, Jack. Maggie's friend. From upstairs. Can I leave a message for her? Yeah? Thanks. Would you just ask her to call me at this number next time you see her? That'd be great. Thank you!" he said before he hung up the phone.

"Maggie?" asked his mum in an inquisitive tone.

"Just a lady I met on the train, Mum. A real nice lady. You'd like her." He smiled.

"In Glasgow?" asked Ida.

"Yeah. She just got a place there." He smiled shyly. *I wouldn't mind staying with her for a while*, he thought. He realized he'd never lived with anyone other than his mum—anyone other than his mum and a few dozen guys in orange. His situation with Maggie seemed much more promising.

"Here; let me finish up those dishes, Mum. You sit down," said Jack as he walked over to the sink. Being helpful really wasn't as difficult as he had always feared it might be. As he washed the dishes, he hummed a little song, stomped his right foot, and had his mum giggling.

Chapter Twenty-Nine

Tuesday morning, 8:30 a.m.

"She just doesn't do what she's supposed to do," Matt muttered under his breath. "If she did, things would be different. All of this would be different." As he spoke, he stood over the lifeless body in front of him. There was blood everywhere. Warm, thick blood that reminded him of gelatin. The body seemed to be floating in a puddle of it. The blood was splattered on the yellow wall on the opposite side of the room as well. *How is that even possible?* he wondered. He'd never shot anyone before. Animals, yes. At far range. But never a human. What surprised him the most, though, was how much he had enjoyed it. In an instant, he had shut her up. And that look of total fear in her eyes as he pointed the trigger at her face was something he would never forget.

The only problem was—it wasn't her. *Who was she?* he wondered. *And how did this strange woman end up at the wrong end of my gun? First things first—let's clean this up. Or let's get out of here. One or the other*, he reasoned.

Matt wrapped his large, calloused hands around Rebecca's delicate ankles as if he didn't want to hurt her. He didn't hate her. He didn't even know her. He tugged. She was heavier than she appeared. More muscular. "Where am I taking you?" he said out loud. "What am I doing? Okay, think, Matt. Think." He dropped her ankles to the ground and looked at his hands. *I'd better get out of here*, he figured. *Get the gun, wipe my prints, as they say in the movies, and leave. No undoing what's been done. So I will run.*

He couldn't find his gun—it had to be here. Tossed on the sofa? Under the worn crocheted blanket on the chair? He couldn't remember. *There it is*, he thought. Tucked under a cushion at the far end of the couch. It was a small handgun he'd been carrying for years. Never fired it before. But it made him feel safer, knowing it was always within reach. In the dresser when he slept. In the glove box of his car. You just never know. He was smart enough to make sure it wasn't registered to him. (Another tip he'd picked up from some movie at some point in this life.) Because you never know. You just never know.

Matt grabbed a blue-striped hand towel from the kitchen and started to wipe down the doorknob, the coffee table, even her ankles. Every step he took, he left a partial footprint—little red marks walking into the kitchen, the hallway, to the end of her body. Now he was down on his knees, wiping frantically, trying to remove any signs of him being there. The more he tried to remove evidence of his presence, the more he seemed to be leaving behind. *Time to go*, he reasoned. Back into the kitchen, he quickly wrapped the doorknob with the soiled towel he'd been carrying, and turned the knob. The door opened to a small backyard with a low fence against the outer edge. Beyond the fence, trees. *This will do*, he thought as he quietly closed the door behind him, checked his coat pocket for his gun, and trotted up to the fence.

Matt managed to get over the fence without getting his pants legs caught. *Now that's an accomplishment*, he thought. *Which way back to the car?* One block over and to the right, he reminded himself. He'd parked at a safe distance, in case things didn't work out. They hadn't. As soon as he reached his car, he tossed his duffle in through the window, climbed in, and locked the door. He just sat there. He looked at the gas gauge—maybe an eighth of a tank—and then at the blood under his fingernails. Blood. *Literally, blood on my hands*, he thought. His face went from a warm shade of pink to beige to white, almost instantly. He unlocked the car door, pushed it open, and leaned out. Everything in his stomach—scrambled eggs, toast, bacon, coffee—came spewing out all over the street in front of him.

Shaking, he wiped the vomit from his face and took a large gulp of cold coffee from the Styrofoam cup he'd earlier left in the car. *Water would've been better*, he thought as he swished the coffee in his mouth and then spit it out on the ground.

Now what? Tilting to the left, he pulled his cell phone out of his back right pocket and started to scroll down. No new messages. There wouldn't be any new messages now. The sender was on the floor, on a pristine white shag carpet now covered in blood. Who was that strange lady? *Damn it, the cell phone! I forgot to get Maggie's cell phone!* Matt put his head into the palms of his hands to quiet the world outside, to give himself a moment to collect his thoughts. Why had Maggie left him anyway? *Where do I go now? Back home? Or do I keep looking for her?*

He looked down at his hands again as they rested on the steering wheel. He still hadn't found Maggie, and now some strange lady was dead. He didn't even remember pulling the trigger, but he knew he had. It was his gun that did it, and his anger that led him there. This wasn't the first time his anger had pushed him to a point of no return, to a moment of temporary vacancy. "Black out anger" was a phrase he'd heard before, and now it made him cringe a bit.

"I'm not going back for the cell phone. I'll just erase the contents." He picked up his phone and took the few steps necessary to delete all the contents of her phone remotely. "Nice. With a few simple commands, I can erase all that. If only life worked like that. And now, I'm going home," Matt declared as he inserted the key in the ignition and slowly turned the wheel to the left. "I don't belong here. Besides, she might be waiting for me at home."

Chapter Thirty

Tuesday evening, 7:45 p.m.

"Phoebe, I think we need some ice cream. To celebrate. What do you think? You coming with?" Maggie called out from the kitchen. She knew if she were going somewhere, anywhere, Phoebe was coming too.

"Yeah, Mom, hold on. Let me get my purse," called Phoebe, who ran back into the bedroom to fetch her brand-new pink sequined coin purse that she'd bought at the grocery store just the day before.

As they made their way down the stairs and into the grocery store, Maggie and Phoebe were greeted by the elderly man behind the counter whose warmth gave them no choice but to smile.

"Hi, Tom," they both called out in response.

"I've got a message for you," Tom replied. "From Jack. You're to call him. Here's his number," he said as he handed Maggie a small yellow Post-it note. "You're welcome to use the phone at the back of the store," he whispered to Maggie.

Maggie and Phoebe headed back to the old black phone and dialed the number. Instantly, Jack's familiar voice answered. And Maggie's heart raced just a bit.

"Hey, Jack."

"Maggie, thanks for calling. How are you? How's Phoebe?"

"All good here. How's your mom?" Maggie asked.

"Oh, she's doing good. Hey, look, I've been thinking about you guys, wondering how you're doing."

"Is everything okay?" asked Maggie, sensing something wasn't being said.

"Yeah. Well, no," interjected Jack. "Remember that lady from the train? The one who was sitting in front of you?"

"Yeah, your friend? The one with the ponytail?" asked Maggie.

"Yeah."

"What about her?" asked Maggie.

Jack stammered a moment. He seemed to be thinking. Or trying to find words. "She...she died."

"What? She died? How? What happened?"

"She got shot. Sometime last night or early this morning. At her parents' house just down the hill from my mum's."

"Oh my God. Who did it?"

"They don't know yet. They don't know anything. A neighbor was walking her dog and saw the front door wide open early this morning. She went inside and found Rebecca dead, with blood all over the place. The only lead is a cell phone they found that wasn't hers. And bloody footprints. Lots of those. But that's it. The whole town is a mess. In shock. Mum too."

Another long pause. Then Jack added, "I shouldn't talk long, Maggie. I'm here with Mum now. I just wanted to let you know I was thinking about you."

Maggie was silent. Her head was swirling. Murder? They just saw her the other day.

"Anyway, I just wanted to make sure you guys were doing okay."

"We're fine. I'm so sorry, Jack. That's horrible."

"Yeah, I know. Look, if you need anything, call me at this number. It's my Mum's."

"Okay, Jack. Thanks."

"I miss you, Mags," he mumbled almost inaudibly just before he hung up.

Maggie stood there for a few moments, elated by Jack's muffled sentiment, yet perplexed by something else. What was it?

"Come on, Phoebe; let's get that ice cream I promised you and head back upstairs." A few minutes later, as they walked up together, Maggie knew something wasn't right. She pulled an ice cream scooper out of the drawer, then stood quietly by the kitchen sink. *Pay attention*, something was telling her. She took two small bowls from the cabinet and placed them on the counter next to the tub of ice cream. *What was it?* she repeated to herself. She filled each of the bowls with two heaping scoops of vanilla ice cream. *What am I not getting?* She mindlessly carried the bowls to the table, then suddenly stopped. The cell phone they found with Rebecca—it was *her* cell phone. She'd almost forgotten that she had dropped it into Rebecca's bag. She had simply been disposing of it, throwing it away. Hadn't thought twice about it. *What does this mean?* she asked herself as a queasy feeling developed in her stomach. The police were assuming this might be their big lead. But it wasn't a lead at all. It was just her cell phone. A coincidence. An accident, really.

Still, something wasn't right about all of this and Maggie knew it. This unsettled feeling followed her throughout the evening, lingering in the bathroom as she bathed Phoebe for the night and sang her a bedtime lullaby. Even as she kissed Phoebe on the forehead and wished her "Sweet dreams," the restless uneasy feeling was there, quietly waiting.

It wasn't often that Maggie got these feelings. In the past, she'd ignore them. She'd push them down. *I just have an overactive imagination*, she'd tell herself, or *Look at who's being too sensitive*, she'd scold. Seemed like she'd spent a lifetime swatting those thoughts away, like little gnats on a hot summer night.

But in retrospect, they'd always been spot on. How many times had she wished she hadn't run from them? This time, however, she decided she would face them—head on.

"This is your mess," a voice inside her whispered. "And you need to clean it up."

Chapter Thirty-One

Thursday morning, 8:30 a.m.

When Maggie was in high school, most of the other girls played basketball. Or volleyball. A few were on the swim team. But Maggie—she ran. She ran track. What she loved most about it was she didn't have to participate, or join in, or think too much about what she was doing. She just had to do what came naturally to her. Run.

She'd slide into her gym shorts, lace up her running shoes, and go. Sometimes, she'd run for miles before she realized how far she'd gone.

With Phoebe in bed for the night and the apartment a bit of a mess, Maggie started to pick up toys scattered on the floor. There weren't many. *One of the advantages to having run away*, Maggie thought. Seemed like she'd always been a runner of some sort. After her mom died, Maggie had run. Not in the sense of going from point A to point B. No, pretty much the opposite. She sat still, shut down, didn't move. She froze. She ran from all the sadness inside of her. She buried it, much like she and Dad buried her mom. Her dad ran to the garage, to his workshop. And she ran to her room. She'd read endless books, fantasies mostly. She never reached out to anyone. In fact, it was years before she ever found the words to express that her mother had died.

But everyone knew. She'd hear them talk in the halls at school.

"Oh, that's the girl who lost her mom last year."

"I heard about that. So sad."

"She's the one?"

"Yeah, that's her. Maggie."

"That sucks."

One crisp, cool autumn afternoon, Maggie walked home slowly from school, head down, eyes studying the fallen leaves on the sidewalk in front of her. She'd kick one to the side only to discover another crispy dry leaf hiding beneath it. She'd kick that to the opposite side and move on to the next. After a block or so of this, she lifted her eyes and wandered home at a slightly more focused pace. When she finally arrived, her father was in the garage, fixing an old carburetor. In the distance, the phone rang. He didn't hear it. A few minutes later, young Maggie appeared with the phone in her hand.

"Dad, it's for you. It's Mrs. Clark, the secretary from school," she said, shrugging as she handed him the phone.

He put his hand over the receiver, and whispered to her, "Is everything okay? Is there something I need to know?"

"Not that I know of, Dad. I promise," she said as she sat on her stool in the corner of the garage, put her head down as if she weren't interested, and listened intently.

"Hello.... Yes, this is Maggie's dad.... Yes, we're doing fine." Putting an end to the obligatory niceties, he asked, "What can I help you with?"

"Oh, I see," Maggie heard him say. After quite a few moments of silence on his end, he continued. "Could be. Okay. Thank you for calling."

He hung up.

"What'd she say, Dad? What did I do?" pleaded Maggie.

"You didn't do anything, Maggie. She was just checking up on you. On us. It's been a tough year for us, you know."

It had been a tough year, and Maggie had slipped away inch by inch.

The next afternoon, when Maggie came home from school, her dad was on the front porch dressed in sweatpants and tennis shoes.

"What's up, Dad? You look silly," she said and laughed.

"I'm going for a run. Care to join me?"

"Oh. Okay, sure."

Maggie trotted upstairs, dug through her laundry basket, and found a dirty set of her gym clothes. Within minutes, she was standing beside her dad out front.

"Let's go," he said as the two of them started a slow jog around the block.

"I didn't know you ran, Dad."

"I don't. Now I do."

"Okay," she said slowly.

"First time out; we won't do too much today," he said as he puffed a bit.

And that's how it started—Maggie's obsession with running. Initially, they'd run together, every night. They'd run about a mile, and then they'd walk a mile.

"What'd you learn today, Maggie?" he'd ask.

"Laws of motion; that's what we're studying now."

"Ah, science. Newton! My favorite," he'd say. "What'd you discover about it?"

"Just objects. And how they go. Or don't go. Seems so simple really."

"Isn't that interesting—how something can seem so simple once it's stated or once it's discovered? Before that moment, though, it's anything but."

"I guess," was her response.

"Some of those laws apply to people too," he said. "I get stuck. I need a push some times."

Maggie playfully shoved him from behind, turning his walk into a trot.

He laughed wholeheartedly.

"Yeah, exactly like that, Maggie," he said as he raced ahead of her.

✦✦✦✦✦✦✦✦

Sometimes, we do need a little push, thought Maggie. On Thursday morning, after dropping Phoebe off at school, Maggie gathered up their clothes, what little they had, and stuffed them in their overnight bag. She turned out the lights in the bedroom. *I'm tired of running.* Maggie sighed. *The last train out of Glasgow leaves right after lunch. And we'll be on it,* she thought as she packed two peanut butter sandwiches, a bag of chips, and an apple. With the few minutes of extra time she had left, she fixed herself a cup of coffee and sat quietly on the sofa. She liked it here. She liked her new home, so simple yet filled with all these new possibilities. She didn't want to leave.

She put her empty cup in the sink, filled it with water, and headed out the door.

Chapter Thirty-Two

Thursday afternoon, 3 p.m.

"As soon as I get one thing fixed, Mum, something else breaks," Jack complained as he followed Ida into the bathroom.

"See, Jack; this cabinet door just doesn't close right."

"No, it doesn't. But that shouldn't be too hard to fix," he said.

"And one more thing," said Ida as she shuffled down the hall to the laundry room. "Something's making a funny noise in here. Hear that?"

He squatted down behind the dryer, loosened the back cover, and nodded.

"I do hear it. Okay, I'll run on down to Hank's and pick up a few parts. Need anything else while I'm out?"

"Nope. Thank you, Jack."

Jack grabbed his jacket and headed out the door. Out of habit, he took the path along the fence rather than the road. He picked a long reed of grass and ran it along the fence, humming a tune from an old cartoon show lodged deeply in his memory.

As he reached the road below, he noticed Sam's car approaching.

"Sam, how's it going?"

Sam slowed down, pulled over, and leaned out the window. "Doing fine; doing just fine for a Thursday morning, Jack. You need a ride somewhere?"

"I'm heading to the hardware store. You going that way?"

They both laughed. In Wolf Point, there really was only one way to go.

"Hop on in, Jack."

Jack opened the car door and climbed in. "Any news about Rebecca's killer?"

"Well, yeah, we just heard something this morning, but mind you, Jack, you can't go blabbing this to everyone. Or anyone, for that matter."

Jack smirked at Sam, thinking this probably wasn't the first time Sam had said that today.

"Mum's the word," was Jack's response.

"They found out who the cell phone belongs to. Some guy in Whitefish."

"Didn't they already know that?" asked Jack.

"Yeah, but now they got a name. Matthew R. McCauley. He's got two phones on his account so they're thinking this one might be his wife's. Or his mother's. Or something." Sam pulled over in front of the hardware store. "They're going to go talk to him, find out what the hell happened."

"Good," said Jack, as he opened the door and stepped out of the police car. "If you hear any more, will you let me know, Sam?"

"You got it, Jack. I will." And off he drove.

McCauley, thought Jack. *That sounds familiar. That kind of sounds like Maggie's last name.* But he had only heard it once so he couldn't be sure. But being from Whitefish, maybe she'd recognize the name. Or maybe she'd know the guy. That was a possibility. *Maybe I'll give her a call tonight*, he thought. Then he chuckled. *You just want to talk to her. You're just looking for an excuse to call her. To keep in touch.* Jack admitted to himself that as much as he liked being home with his mum, he really did miss Maggie. He missed little Phoebe too.

Yeah, I'll call her when I get back to Mum's, he decided.

Chapter Thirty-Three

Thursday afternoon, 3 p.m.

Why was it that the trip back always seemed to take so much longer than the trip there? Didn't even matter where you were going or where you'd been. Must be the anticipation of things to come, Matt supposed. Because prior to, anything and everything was possible. He'd hoped he'd be bringing his wife and his baby home. That was his plan.

That wasn't what had happened. He was returning to an empty house, and on one level, he knew this. But deep down inside, he silently wished he'd be proven wrong—that someone would be waiting for him, just this once.

As Matt turned down his street, he noticed immediately that someone was waiting for him. But it wasn't who he was hoping for.

Chapter Thirty-Four

Thursday evening, 6 p.m.

Jack opened the front door and announced his arrival.

"Mum?" he called out loudly. No answer. She must've gone to town. Or maybe she was in the garden. He sauntered through the house straight to the kitchen, poured himself a tall glass of milk, and snatched three cookies from the glass cookie jar.

He sat down at the table and reached for the phone.

"Hey, Tom. Yeah, Jack here. Can I leave another message for Maggie?"

"Haven't seen her yet today, Jack. Usually by this time, I woulda seen both of them half a dozen times."

"Ask her to call me when you do see her. Okay?"

"Sure. No problem."

"We'll get cell phones next week," said Jack, laughing. He figured it was about time to join the rest of the world.

As Jack headed from the kitchen back to his bedroom, he started thinking about Maggie and this Matthew McCauley guy in Whitefish. *Maybe I'll head over to the library*, he thought. *Practice some of my new research skills that I've been honing these past four years.*

Like everything else in Wolf Point, the library was just a quick trip down the path and a sharp turn to the left. Both of the desktop computers in the back of the small one-room building were available. Jack scooted up his chair and started clicking away. M A T T H E W M C C A U L E Y M I S S O U L A. No Facebook page, but an address popped up instantly, along with a short list of relatives. Top of the list: Margaret McCauley.

Okay, this is getting weird, thought Jack.

He jotted down Matthew's address and phone number, stuck the piece of paper in the front pocket of his jacket, and headed back home.

After preparing a home-cooked dinner of rice and beans with just a touch of Cajun pepper, Jack carefully set the table with two plastic bowls, paper napkins on the left, and spoons on the right. Then he sat down and picked up the phone again.

"I still haven't seen her, Jack. You sure she's not headed your way?" asked Tom.

"Yeah, positive. Thanks, Tom."

Jack sat quietly for a moment and then picked up the phone again.

"Hey, Sally. Just wondering if Maggie made it to work today."

"She didn't show, Jack. I had to work a double. Still am." Sally sighed.

"Okay, thanks," said Jack, but the line went dead before he could hang up. Betty was obviously really busy. He placed the phone back on its cradle, then got up and wandered into the living room where his mother was watching *Jeopardy*.

"Mum, dinner's ready," Jack announced.

As Ida followed Jack back to the table, she said, "Sure smells good, Jack. You're going to make some lady a nice husband one day." She chuckled.

"Doubt that," said Jack. "Hey, Mum, I can't reach Maggie."

"You called her?" Ida asked.

"A few times, Mum. No one's seen her at her apartment."

"Is this like her? Is she flighty?" asked Ida.

"No, not at all. She didn't show up for work either."

"Oh, that doesn't sound good, Jack. How well do you know her?"

"Mum, I know her. I know her well enough to know something's not right."

They sat quietly at the table for a moment, each mentally going to their own dark places.

"I'm pretty sure she's running from her husband, Mum, with her daughter Phoebe."

"How old's Phoebe?"

"Five. She's so cute, Mum. You'd love her."

"Husband's an asshole?"

Jack nodded. He knew his mom had known a few in her time. At least one anyway. So there wasn't much more Jack needed to say.

"Sometimes running away is the bravest thing a woman can do," said Ida.

Jack sometimes wondered if his mom had wished she'd done things differently, wished she hadn't tried so hard to make things work. Neither one of them said anything for a few minutes. Jack moved his rice and beans around and around his plate with his fork. Ida took a few little bites.

"Maybe you should go check on her?" Ida's anxious voice shattered the silence. "Catch the train down tomorrow?"

"Maybe. But I got a feeling she might've headed back where she came from. To Whitefish."

"Why?"

"Can't say for sure, Mum. Just a feeling. And no one's seen her all day in Glasgow. I am worried about her. And her daughter."

"Oh, Jack, I'm sorry."

The silence returned. Ida stirred her rice and beans slowly, as if to let them cool. She took a long, slow sip of her water. After what seemed like minutes, she broke the silence again.

"Take my car, Jack."

"What?"

"I've got groceries. Nowhere I need to be for a few days. And it sounds like there's somewhere you need to be."

"That's crazy, Mum."

"It's not, Jack."

"I haven't driven since that night."

"You'll be fine," she said confidently.

Without much more thought, Jack asked, "You sure, Mum?"

"I'm sure, Jack. Help yourself to it. It's got gas. And there's a little money in the glove box if you need more."

Jack smiled. His mum wasn't just giving him her keys. He knew this. She was offering him her trust, something he had broken years ago. A deep warmth radiated throughout his body as he looked over at his mum. She trusted him. He stood, walked over to her, and hugged her so hard it could've shattered her. But it didn't.

For the first time in his life, Jack had an overwhelming sense of clarity. Of purpose. He headed back to his childhood bedroom, a room that suddenly seemed too small, as if he had just outgrown it. He packed up his backpack and set it by his bedroom door. He wasn't exactly sure what he was doing or why, but he felt like he had no choice but to go.

Chapter Thirty-Five

Thursday afternoon, 4 p.m.

Matt drove by his house without looking directly at it. Nonchalantly. Out of the corner of his eye, he observed the cop car out front and noted instantly that there were two cops sitting in it, literally watching his house. *It didn't take them long to get here,* thought Matt. *Just two days.*

Where to now? I could run, but that's exactly what they'd think I'd be doing. I'll give them time to wait, to look around, and to conclude that I'm not coming back. How to outfox the fox? Matt smirked.

Besides, what they really don't know about me is this: This is my house. And I'm not leaving. Matt kept driving slowly. He pulled into an empty driveway up the hill, overlooking his backyard. No one was around. His neighbors who lived there were gone for the month, visiting their grandkids. He knew this. Matt sat in his car, waiting patiently. Whether the hunter or the hunted, he knew the drill. After an hour or so, when the cop car drove away, Matt grabbed his bag, got out of the car, and headed down the hill to the barn.

They'll be back soon, hoping to find me here. To question. Or possibly with a search warrant, Matt thought. He opened the barn door, closing it carefully behind him. He made his way to the back, where the hay lay thickly on the ground. There was a stable in here for a horse, but no horse. Plenty of room for chickens or pigs, too. But none of those either. He kicked some hay to the side to expose an old wooden door on the floor. He pulled the latch up, and a set of old ladder-like steps appeared. He climbed his way down below the floor of the barn. After a few minutes, he reappeared, climbed back up, and carefully shut the floor door. *There. At least they won't find my gun now.* With his right foot, he scattered hay across the top of it, hiding any signs of what lay below. He quickly headed out the door and back up the hill.

Within an hour or two, just as he'd anticipated, the cop car returned. This time, though, the two officers got out of their car and headed to the door of Matt's house. *Must've gotten the search warrant*, thought Matt as he crouched down farther in his car on the hill. He knew they couldn't see him, wouldn't even think to look way up here anyway, but he found comfort in the act of hunkering down. *I'll give them an hour*, he calculated. *That's probably all they'll need to find whatever they're looking for.* He checked his watch. *What they're really looking for*, he admitted, *is me. Good luck with that, boys.* He chuckled to himself.

Chapter Thirty-Six

Thursday evening, 8 p.m.

Jack held the small black Tracfone in his hand. He turned it on, then off again. He turned it over. He put it in his pocket, then pulled it out again. *My first cell phone*, thought Jack proudly. He did have to borrow the money from his mum to buy it, but still—quite an accomplishment. He'd texted his new number to Sam. "If you hear anything, Sam, let me know. Text me at this number." He smiled. He left his number for his mum, too, on a little sheet of note paper by the phone at the house.

With his cell phone in his pocket and his hands on the steering wheel, Jack stopped for a moment and breathed deeply. Driving and owning a phone were things other twenty-three-year-olds might take for granted, but not Jack. He'd lost a bit of time, but in some respects, he'd gained something else. Appreciation, maybe? And the feeling of being free. Not free in the sense of being lost and rudderless, but rather free in being able to make choices, to choose to help other people if he wanted to, to go places he'd never been. For once in his life, Jack no longer felt stuck.

He shifted the car into gear, pulled out slowly, and was on his way.

Chapter Thirty-Seven

Friday morning, 7 a.m.

Maggie had always wanted to take Phoebe on a train trip, but one on Monday and another three days later on Thursday? A bit much for Maggie, but Phoebe was thrilled. Even better, they'd spent the night in a hotel in Whitefish.

As Phoebe slept in, Maggie hit replay in her mind, sorting through the events of the last few days. Right now, she didn't really have a plan. Just a direction. Okay, maybe it was more of a gut reaction than a direction.

And possibly an overreaction? *I do need a phone*, she admitted. *My own phone. I shouldn't have cut out on everyone. Especially on Jack. I didn't have to run. Because, once again, in an attempt to not run, I ran.*

If it's my mess, I'll clean it up, she promised herself as she started to gather the clothing they'd tossed on the floor the night before. She must've been more tired than she realized, she thought as she picked up the remains of their burgers and fries scattered about the bedside table and dresser.

"Mom," Phoebe's waking voice rose from under the covers, "that was so much fun. We should eat popcorn in bed every night."

Maggie laughed. What was it about hotel rooms and the tossing aside of hard, fast rules? She remembered her dad letting her jump on hotel beds and eat popcorn while watching TV, too.

"Are we going home today, Mom? I want Dad to teach me how to ride a bike. He said he would. He promised."

"I think we're going to start the day with a visit to Mrs. Dorothy. How about that? She's really missed you, too."

Phoebe shrieked. "Mrs. Dorothy. I miss her, Mommy."

Phoebe jumped out of bed and grabbed her jeans and sweater from the pile of dirty clothes. She brushed her teeth as quickly as possible. Within what seemed like minutes, they were headed out the door.

"Phoebe, I don't think you need your coat today. I'll carry it for you," said Maggie as they stepped out into one of those unseasonably warm winter days in Montana. *That's the thing about living here*, considered Maggie. *This time of year, you never know what you're going to get. So you have to be ready for anything.*

The trees that lined both sides of Second Avenue were still in winter mode, despite the warm weather. Bare birch trees on one side, and ancient elms on the other. As Maggie and Phoebe neared the end of Second Avenue, they saw Dorothy's old bungalow-style house tucked neatly behind an overgrown hedge. How did Dorothy become such a friend to Phoebe? Maggie couldn't quite remember. Possibly from their daily walks around the neighborhood. Just as Maggie expected on a warm day like today, Mrs. Dorothy was on the porch, wrapped in a blanket, swinging slowly on the porch swing. As soon as she spotted Maggie and Phoebe, she stood up and clapped her hands in excitement.

"A sight for sore eyes!" She walked down the first two steps.

"Mrs. Dorothy! Mrs. Dorothy!" Phoebe raced up the stairs with her arms wide open. She clutched on lovingly to the large older woman's left leg. In anticipation, Mrs. Dorothy had braced herself by holding on tightly to the stair rail.

"Such big love from such a small child!" exclaimed Dorothy. "Oh, my goodness, how have you two been? Haven't seen you around in days. Thought maybe you were sick or something."

"No, Phoebe and I headed out of town for a bit. Just to get away."

"Where'd you go?"

"We took the train. To Glasgow. Ever been there?"

"Yeah, my sister lives there. I took the train there about five years ago. For Thanksgiving. Pretty place. Nice and quiet."

"Yeah, I like it there. I could see living there."

"You thinking of moving, Maggie?" asked Mrs. Dorothy. She had a way of staying out of someone's business without staying out of their business.

"I don't know," whispered Maggie.

Mrs. Dorothy put her hand on Maggie's shoulder. "Cute little town. Good school, too. My sister was a substitute teacher there for a little while."

"Sometimes a change seems like a good idea. Know what I mean?" asked Maggie, in search of validation.

"How are things at home?" Mrs. Dorothy asked cautiously. Their conversations tended to float on the surface, but it seemed like Maggie needed to talk.

"I don't know."

They sat quietly for a few moments. Then Mrs. Dorothy started talking. She was good at that.

"Ralph and I—things weren't always good," said Mrs. Dorothy. "There was a time when things were downright awful. He'd get to drinking. He'd get all angry like. Mostly, I'd just steer clear of him when he'd get like that. But sometimes, he'd be looking for a fight. And he'd come looking for me."

"I didn't know."

"No, I don't talk about it much. No need to really. But one time, he was really drunk. He knocked me down good. Broke my arm. Had to wear a cast for weeks."

"Oh God, I didn't know."

"He never did it again, though."

"How'd you get him to stop?"

"I shot his ass. Buried him out back. That's why you never met him."

Maggie stared blankly at Mrs. Dorothy.

"Oh, good Lord, Maggie, I'm pulling your leg. Yeah, he did break my arm. But he never drank again after that. I think maybe he knew I just might shoot him if it happened again."

Maggie laughed. Mrs. Dorothy was a surprise. Underneath all her well-worn, grandmotherly love and charm, there was spunk. Admirable spunk. No wonder Maggie usually meandered over this way on her daily walks with Phoebe. *A little of this rubbing off wouldn't be a bad thing at all*, thought Maggie.

"Would you mind horribly if I left Phoebe here with you for just a few hours?" asked Maggie. "I've got a few errands to run."

"Mind? Are you kidding me? There's nothing I would love more. Just take your time, Maggie!"

Maggie smiled as she gave Phoebe a quick kiss on the top of her head.

"You be good now," mocked Phoebe, in anticipation of the words already forming on her mother's lips.

Maggie smiled. "Okay, have fun then. Is that better?"

Phoebe laughed and held Mrs. Dorothy's hand as the two old friends walked into the house together.

And now, I've got the rest of the morning and maybe afternoon, thought Maggie as she headed back down Second. As she approached her old neighborhood, she slowed down, taking the time to recognize every tree, every bush along the way. She noticed the same divots in the roughly worn pavement, the large rocks that bordered one side, the overgrown shrubs on the others. *Hundreds of*

late afternoons spent pushing a stroller along this bumpy road, thought
Maggie. Funny, it had only been a week since her last stroll down
this lane, but it felt like a lifetime.

Was it really that bad? she wondered. Was she justified in abruptly running away and taking Phoebe with her? She slowed her pace
for a moment. Marriage is forever. It should be, anyway. That's what
her father would say. "Pick a good one, Maggie. Pick one that'll
last a lifetime." Was Matt really so bad? Her mind drifted to the
better times, the softer moments. That sunny afternoon the three of
them spent down at the river. They'd packed a lunch of pesto pasta,
cheese and crackers, and fresh fruit salad. And brought a blanket to
sit on. The sun was shining—not a cloud in the sky. Nothing had
gone wrong. That's what made that one afternoon so memorable.
There were no angry outbursts or tears. Just a peaceful afternoon at
the river. *That, dear Maggie, was the exception*, she reminded herself.
*You left for a good reason. And you've come back for an even better
one—something horrible happened to that lady, that friend of Jack's.
And it might've had something to do with your cell phone. You have to
stop running. You have to find out what happened. You somehow have
to make this right, Maggie.* She could hear her father's voice inside
her head. "You cannot keep running away."

The thought of confronting Matt, though, just the thought of
it, made Maggie feel nauseous. Confronting anyone made her nervous. But Matt? The closer Maggie got to her house, the more she
felt like throwing up. And retreating.

As she turned the corner, she stopped. "What the hell…?" she
gasped. Right in front of her house was a police car. And at her front
door, two officers waiting for someone to answer their knocks.

"Oh, this cannot be good," she whispered as she turned abruptly back in the direction she had just come from. *What is going on?* she wondered. A police car. But no ambulance, so that was good. No sirens. But still. The thought of approaching the officers and asking what was happening never occurred to her. Run, Maggie. Run. That was her motto. After a few blocks, she slowed down just a bit and caught her breath. Shortly after, the police car passed her. She didn't look up. She kept her head down and continued walking until the car turned the corner and was out of sight. She stopped for a moment, then turned back around and headed toward her house.

She walked up to the front door and stood there for a moment. *You can do this, Maggie,* she told herself. She knew the door wouldn't be locked. It was never locked. There was no lock. Never had been. She turned the handle and stepped inside. Silence. She wandered from the front hall to the kitchen, walking slowly, quietly. Looking for something, although she wasn't sure what. *Where is Matt?* she wondered. No sign of him in the house. *Why were the police here?* She didn't know that either. From the kitchen to the pantry to the living room. Nothing. She stood at the bottom of the staircase and caught her breath. Listened for a moment. And started up, slowly, step by step. To the master bedroom door. She opened it quietly, thoughtfully, as if not to wake anyone who might be sleeping inside. She tiptoed to the nightstand by Matt's side of the bed and slowly opened the drawer. It creaked. She stopped. Waited. Then opened it more. She pulled out the handgun she knew would be there, duct-taped to the top of the inside of the drawer where no one would find it, and held it carefully with both hands. She slid the drawer closed again and softly shut the bedroom door on her way out.

She went back downstairs to the living room and sat. She waited. She could hardly breathe. *Breathe, Maggie, breathe*, she kept telling herself. She knew he'd return. Eventually. This was his house. He'd be back.

Chapter Thirty-Eight

Friday morning, 9:30 a.m.

All clear, thought Matt as he watched the cop car pull away. *They didn't go in my house. I'm guessing that means no search warrant. Not yet anyway. They'll be back.* He stepped out of his car and quietly closed the car door. *They need to find me to question me. So I stay hidden. No one will see my car here*, he reassured himself as he walked back down the hill to the barn.

Inside the barn, there were signs of disturbance that only Matt would notice. A shovel turned the wrong way, a blanket folded incorrectly. Imagined? Matt wasn't sure. All in all, though, it was fine. They hadn't found anything. They didn't even know where to look. Or what they were looking for.

From the barn, he headed to the house, entering through the back door, stepping into the kitchen. Everything here seemed in order. From the kitchen to the stairs. He walked slowly through every room, carefully observing. Phoebe's room. Untouched. Bathrooms. Pristine. He cracked opened the door to the master bedroom. All good. Back down the stairs, from the rear of house, down the hall to the living room. He stopped. He saw her, sitting there waiting for him. Just as she should be.

"Hello, Maggie," he said calmly.

"Hello, Matt," she replied.

He could tell instantly that she was nervous. Her voice was shaking. *That's good*, he thought. *She should be. She's out of her league here.*

"Where have you been, Maggie?"

"Have you been tracking me, Matt?" Her voice was shaking. "Did you follow my cell phone?"

"Maggie, where did you go?"

"A woman was murdered. Do you know anything about that?"

By now, he was standing over her.

"I'm not going to keep asking, Maggie. Where did you go?"

Maggie started crying. He wasn't answering her question. "I left. I had to leave."

"Why Maggie? Why did you leave?" He stepped closer.

"Did you go get my cell phone?"

"Why did you leave?"

She started crying harder. "I had to."

"Why?"

"Did you murder Rebecca? Did you, Matt? Did you kill her?"

"Rebecca," he said calmly. He repeated it slowly. "Rebecca."

"Did you kill her?" She sobbed.

"Did she have your phone, Maggie?"

Maggie held her head with her hands and sobbed.

"Why did she have your phone, Maggie?"

Suddenly, it felt like it was all her fault. She had slipped her cell phone into Rebecca's bag. How could she have? What had she been thinking? Was she ultimately responsible for Rebecca's death?

Matt was so close that he was almost touching her.

"Maggie, why did she have your phone? Did you give her your phone?"

Maggie just cried. She couldn't stop crying long enough to answer. She wouldn't have known what to say anyway. She hadn't meant for anything to happen. Never thought anything would come of it. She just didn't want the phone anymore. Didn't want the phone—and all that it was attached to. But she couldn't tell that to Matt. No, that would just make everything worse. So much worse. So she cried instead.

He seemed to be all around her, suffocating her. She stood up and stepped back, as if for air. And that infuriated him. He grabbed her by the shoulders, lifted her two inches off the ground, and started to shake her.

The gun she was hiding fell to the floor.

He grabbed it and struck her across the face with it. Hard.

"No!" He stopped himself. "No, no, no," he said out loud as he took five steps back. "This cannot happen again. There just isn't room," he scolded himself.

Chapter Thirty-Nine

Friday morning, 9:00 a.m.

The sun was shining. The sky was blue. And Jack had managed to find a well-timed truck stop along the way where he pulled over and slept through most of the night. Driving down the interstate, singing loudly, Jack figured he was making pretty good time. *Okay, enough of my voice*, he thought as he reached over to turn on the radio. Wouldn't you know it? There was his song. His and Chad's song. *How funny*, he thought, *that it would be playing now*. For some reason, most nights when they had gone out, this song would be on the radio. Or they'd be walking down Main, right past a store, and they could hear it seeping out through the windows. They'd sing along, acting it out, exaggerating the emotions behind it as kids will do.

Jack reached over and turned off the radio. *Too much*, he thought. Too much right now. He felt an ache inside that never really went away. Somehow, this had become their song. Hearing it now made Jack miss Chad even more. It was the silly times he missed the most.

Those moments when only those two "got it." And everyone else was an outsider who just didn't. Or couldn't.

Jack had never had a little brother, but he imagined his connection with Chad had been what that would've been like. Hell, they'd basically grown up together. They had known things about each other that no one else knew. Dirty, dark little secrets. Like if you brought up who Chad's parents liked better—him or his sister—he'd go ballistic. And if you kept at it, he'd start crying. Or what actually happened to his grandmother's diamond ring. He'd lost it somewhere in the woods, but managed to make it look like Rebeca had taken it. No one knew this, except for Chad. And Jack. That's just the way it was. And the same was true for Chad. He knew where all of Jack's buttons were, and just for fun, he'd push them sometimes. He also knew about those quiet little truths that never see the light of day, the ones that get buried in the closet or in the backyard or deep within our souls. Like how Jack always had a bottle of something in the back of his closet or under his bed. And how freaked out he'd get if his stash got low. Because of this—because of this sharing of a lifetime of secrets—there was a trust. A trust that resulted in a thick layer of fierce protection. No one was more protective of Chad than Jack. No secret there. You didn't mess with Chad unless you wanted to mess with Jack. Period.

Why the hell did Chad have to die? Jack slammed his palms against the steering wheel. What if they hadn't taken Chad's dad's car that night? What if they'd walked like they always did? Or gotten to the party a little earlier? Or stayed a little later? Five minutes either way might've changed everything. Jack found himself trying to rethink that night, trying to change the outcome on something that had happened more than four years ago. *All the thinking in the world isn't going to change what happened*, Jack reminded himself. And then he could hear his cellmate's voice inside his head: "Accept it, or go mad, Jack. Those are your choices."

Jack sighed deeply and wiped a tear from his eye. This kind of thinking wasn't helping. "I'm tired of thinking, of singing, and I don't want to listen to the radio," he said defiantly. "Must be time to eat," he figured. "And stretch." He pulled over at a dusty old truck stop. He got out of the car, stood stiffly, and stretched his long lanky self. "Shake it off," he told himself. "The past is the past. The present is a gift. And lack of food is making you cranky, Jack."

He leaned to the left, to the right, and stretched backwards as far as he could. He shook his head from side to side, and then strolled confidently into the diner, where he landed firmly on the first stool available.

"I'll have a burger and a Coke," he said a bit loudly. He'd never been on a road trip alone before. Actually, he'd never been on a road trip period. He pulled out his phone and checked for messages. A thumbs-up from Sam. Nothing else. But no one else knew he had this phone.

Starting over is a funny business, thought Jack. We can start a day over at any time, and we can start a life over too. Kind of. Getting out was like starting over. In some ways, it was like the world had evolved without him in it. Everyone had moved on, grown up, gotten a life, lived. Not Jack. He had been on hold for four years, and now, now he had some catching up to do.

"How'd you want that burger cooked?" asked the waitress as she set an ice-cold Coke down in front of Jack. She had short black hair, red lips, and a perky little smile.

"Well done'll do it," said Jack.

She smiled.

He could tell she kind of liked him. She was hanging around this end of the counter more than the other. Jack felt a little rusty, out of practice. Not that he'd ever had the chance to get much practice at this sort of thing. At least not where he'd been these past few years.

"Hey, miss, a little service down this way please," said a heavy guy, smirking from down the counter.

"Good times," the waitress muttered under her breath as she winked at Jack. "Coming big guy," she told the impatient customer.

Jack smiled. *I don't ever want to get locked up again*, he thought. *There's too much out here I've been missing. Ordering burgers, smiling at waitresses, singing down the highway, helping friends.* After he finished eating, which took a grand total of five minutes, he reached into his pocket and pulled out his wallet. Out came a crisp twenty-dollar bill, which was more than enough to cover it. It was easy to feel generous with someone else's money. He laughed, promising himself he would pay his mum back for all of this, even the tip. He nodded politely at the waitress and headed back to his car. Just as he finished filling up the tank, he got a call from Sam.

"Hey, Jack, how's it going?"

"Going good. What's up, Sam?"

"So this Matthew guy, the one in Whitefish," Sam started saying, as if he'd just paused for a moment and was now continuing his sentence.

"Yeah?" asked Jack.

"They went to his house and he wasn't there."

"Do they have any idea where he is?" Jack figured Sam had been carrying on a conversation with Jack all morning, even though Jack wasn't there. All in Sam's head. But honestly, Jack was just happy that he was part of this particular conversation. He wanted to be on the receiving end of this information dump.

"No idea yet. They'll check back again. They're kind of hanging around the place till the search warrant comes through."

"So it was his phone?" asked Jack.

"Either his or his wife's. She wasn't home either. Asking around the neighborhood and no one's seen her for a week or two. That might not mean anything. She didn't get out and about a lot."

I've got a pretty good idea where she might've been, Jack thought. He had just been on the train with her the last few days, running away from her husband. Although he didn't know that at the time. She had clearly avoided mentioning Matthew or a husband or anything of the sort. Jack scratched his head.

"The other thing," said Sam.

"What?" asked Jack, a little unsure what the first thing was.

"He was living with someone prior to this wife. Seven or so years ago. A woman named Lisa."

"Yeah?"

"Seems she just kind of disappeared," said Sam.

"What do you mean?"

"I called the place where she used to work. Talked to her manager at the time. She said she didn't remember much about Lisa. She was the type who'd come to work, do her job, go home. Then one day, she didn't come to work."

"And?" asked Jack, not quite following.

"So, the job called the guy she was living with—this Matthew guy. He said she'd gone off to visit her sick mom, but she never came back. Jack, I did some checking. Both of her parents had been dead for at least ten years. Makes no sense."

"No one went looking for her?" asked Jack.

"No. She just kind of disappeared. Can't imagine anything sadder than that. She just kind of disappeared," said Sam. "And then was quickly forgotten."

Jack could almost hear Sam rubbing the top of his head.

"I'd rather be remembered as an asshole than not at all," said Sam.

Jack nodded. *Or as a drunk*, thought Jack. *Even that would be better.*

"Well, thanks for listening, Jack," said Sam. "I'll keep you in the loop. I know Rebecca meant the world to you."

"Yeah, she did." Jack nodded thoughtfully as he hung up.

Jack placed his cell phone carefully on the dash, started the engine, and headed back onto the interstate. *What was Maggie's part in all of this?* he wondered. It was her husband's cell phone that the cops had found next to the body of a dead woman. His best friend's sister's dead body. He rubbed his temples thoughtfully. Somehow, somehow everything was connected. He knew this. And he couldn't help feeling that Maggie was in some kind of trouble. Or danger. Or both.

Chapter Forty

When she was five, Maggie was invincible. No one could fly down that old dirt hill on McClay Flats like she could. And her brand-new bike made her even more fearless. She'd pick up speed, tuck her head down, and soar. What happened that one time, though? She hit a bump. Or a rut. That's what her father had said. All she remembered was tumbling over the handlebars and landing smack on her face. She lay there for quite a while, waiting. Surrounded by the musky, clean earthy smell of dirt, there was an initial moment of calm. Of peace almost. Maggie lay there quietly, assessing her situation, feeling her limbs, checking for pain. But slowly, the gentle numbness gave way to throbbing. And the sweet, comforting smell of dirt was replaced with the metallic taste of blood.

Twenty-three years later, Maggie found herself surrounded by that familiar smell again. Earthy, clean, cold. This time, though, she couldn't see anything. There was only darkness. She couldn't move. Her hands were tied tightly behind her back. And there was something stuffed in her mouth. She suddenly realized she was blind-folded, gagged, and tied to a chair.

Within moments, that sweet smell of dirt was replaced with an unbearable throbbing in her head. And a paralyzing fear in her heart.

Did Matt do this? Did he honestly do this to me? she wondered. He had a temper, yes. He'd always had a temper. But she had never really believed he was capable of more than merely harsh, biting words. Before now, he'd never actually hit her. He'd threatened to. Numerous times. He'd raised the back of his hand as if. But he'd always stopped, just before striking.

Not this time, though. He had struck her across her face with the butt of his gun. *Was he capable of this?* she asked herself again. And if so, then what else could he be capable of? She didn't answer her second question. She didn't need to.

"I've got to get out of here," her muffled voice whispered.

Chapter Forty-One

Friday morning, 10:30 a.m.

So, this is Whitefish, thought Jack as he pulled off of I-93 and onto East Second Street. Old homes, Victorian style, quaint. On the surface, that's what people see. But underneath? Leaky faucets, broken pipes, fences in need of repair. He smiled. Job security at every turn. He drove past the hospital, over the river. He reached into the front pocket of his jacket and pulled out the crumpled piece of paper he had stuffed in there days ago: Park Avenue. Only a few miles away. *How did people survive before GPS?* he wondered. A GPS for directions in life would be kind of nice. He laughed at the thought. He knew where he was, but he wasn't entirely sure where he was going.

Within minutes, Jack found himself turning onto Park. As he drove by the front of the house that belonged to Matthew and Margaret McCauley, he admitted that he had no clue what he was hoping to find. For starters, was anyone home? No car was parked out front. He couldn't tell if there was one in the garage either. But honestly, he wouldn't even know what kind of car he was looking for. What kind of car would Maggie drive anyway?

Nor was the house on Park Avenue the kind of house Jack would've pictured Maggie in. No clean white shutters on the windows. No picket fence. No warm, welcoming front porch. This house was more rustic, more manly. It had a "stay away" look to it. He didn't see any toys or plastic dollhouses scattered about the yard. Nothing but pinecones and dead grass. Maggie's house? That just didn't seem to fit.

Who was this Maggie McCauley? Jack wondered. *Outside of her life on the train or her tiny existence in Glasgow, who was this woman he was on his way to rescue? And why did she need rescuing?*

"I could sit here for hours and wait for something to happen," Jack told himself. "Or I could go get myself a cup of coffee." Infinite patience was not Jack's strong suit. "Coffee it is," he said as he shifted into gear and started off toward town.

An old '50s-style diner in a building desperately in need of repair. Now this is my kind of place, thought Jack as he pulled open the full-glass front door and walked in. Only one customer inside, an elderly man sitting at the counter slowly sipping on a cup of coffee. *Looks like he might've been sipping on that coffee for hours.*

"What can I getcha?" asked the waitress before Jack had a chance to plant himself on the stool.

"Cup of coffee and a cheese Danish would be nice."

"You got it," she said as she scribbled something illegible on a piece of paper and handed it to the cook.

She turned Jack's coffee mug right side up and filled it to the top. It had the smell of coffee that had been heating on the pot for hours.

"Thanks. Smells good."

"Welcome. Haven't seen you here before," she said.

"I'm new to town. Just visiting some friends of mine. Maggie McCauley. You know her?"

The waitress paused for a moment.

"Yeah, I do. She's not a regular. Never been in here. Not that I know of. But I see her from time to time. She and that cute little girl of hers usually go walking by here in the morning. On their way to Mrs. Dorothy's."

"Mrs. Dorothy's?"

"Yeah, over on Second. That old lady attracts more kids than anyone I've ever known. They just gather at her house like little rodents." She laughed.

Jack smiled. "On Second, you said?"

"Yeah, just a few streets over. She used to be a nurse, you know. Mrs. Dorothy. I've seen her out front, fixing up bumps and scratches. She must like taking care of everyone."

"Ding. Order up," came from the little window separating the kitchen from the dining room. The waitress turned and picked up the white porcelain plate with a cheese Danish plopped on it.

"There you go. Let me know if I can getcha anything else." She set the small plate down in front of him.

"Thanks."

"You know, I haven't seen those two—Maggie and that little girl of hers—all week. Just realized that," she said without expecting an answer.

Jack ate his Danish in silence, following every bite with another swig of coffee. Once done, he left a handful of bills on the counter, nodded politely, and headed out the door.

"Where to now, Jack?" he asked himself as he slithered into the car. He quickly checked his phone again. Nothing. "Okay, back to Maggie's house," he said to himself as he started up the car.

Jack took a sharp right, back onto Park Avenue, and drove by Maggie's house again. Nothing new here. Unsure of what to do next, Jack decided to wander. He turned onto Second, a picturesque street shaded by ancient elms and oaks. Just as the snow was starting to give way to the soft green underbelly, front doors were opening, releasing children who had been stored inside all winter. Jack passed a group of kids laughing and playing. He watched as they formed frosty white balls with the last remnants of snow and launched them at one another. Driving ever so slowly, Jack took the next right on Second. *Definitely the older part of town,* he thought. *Maybe people grow old in the homes they were born in. This neighborhood had that sense about it.* As he reached the cul-de-sac at the end of the street, he saw a little girl who reminded him of Phoebe. He missed her. Messy long hair and a certain tilt to her stance.

As he got closer, Jack realized it was Phoebe. He stopped. She looked up at his car as it slowed, saw his face, and stopped too. She smiled. She didn't seem a bit surprised, though, as if it were normal that Jack would be here. He chuckled. *The beautiful simplicity of a child's mind*, he thought. *"Well, of course here's Jack, randomly visiting me in a place he's never been to. This is my world, and Jack is a part of it. Period."* Jack pulled over and stepped out of the car. He walked over to the white picket fence, reached over, and lifted Phoebe up to give her a hug. She melted into him. An older woman with soft gray hair and a warm round face came waddling quickly down the front porch steps.

"Phoebe!" she roared.

Jack instantly set Phoebe back down, realizing this woman must be the Mrs. Dorothy the waitress had mentioned. And maybe this Mrs. Dorothy didn't like strangers picking up her little Phoebe. *Understandable*, thought Jack as he quickly introduced himself.

"I'm Jack."

Mrs. Dorothy came closer. "I'm guessing you're a friend of Phoebe's?" she asked suspiciously.

"Yes, and Maggie's," Jack replied.

"I'm Mrs. Dorothy," she said as she wiped her hands on her apron and extended one over the fence in a welcoming gesture.

"Didn't expect to run into Phoebe," said Jack. "Is Maggie here?"

"No, she's running some errands, so she left little Phoebe with me. Come on in," she said as she opened the fence's gate. "Any friend of Phoebe's," she added as her suspicion gave way to curiosity, "is a friend of mine."

Phoebe smiled proudly as she led Jack around the yard.

"We buried Butch here. Butch isn't a dog. He's a cat. He died." She frowned. Five steps farther, she said, "And this is where the roly-poly bugs come every spring. Right, Mrs. Dorothy?"

"Yes, dear."

"This little tree, see this one?" Phoebe asked with excitement.

"Yeah. It's pretty, Phoebe," Jack replied.

"I planted it. When I come to visit, I get to water it. That's my job," Phoebe said proudly.

"It almost died, Phoebe. I had to step in and water it for you when you were gone," scolded Mrs. Dorothy, hoping to get a few more details from her little friend.

"We were on a train. Right, Jack?" said Phoebe.

"Oh?" Mrs. Dorothy's asked. "Where were you going?"

Phoebe was silent, as if searching for the answer. She didn't know. And Jack wasn't about to divulge any information he wasn't supposed to.

"Any idea when Maggie might be back?" he asked as a way of changing the subject. He figured the less people knew right now, the better. At least until he got a chance to talk to Maggie about what was really going on.

"She said just a few hours. You're welcome to wait for her here if you'd like," said Mrs. Dorothy.

"Thank you. I appreciate that. But I've got a few things to take care of myself while I'm here," Jack replied. "I'll see you in a bit, Ms. Phoebe." He patted her on the head and then headed to the gate. He imagined the next few hours might be filled with lots of questions for Phoebe now that Mrs. Dorothy's need-to-know had been piqued. *Time for me to get out of here*, thought Jack as he took longer steps than usual, heading to the car.

So Maggie was alive. She was here in Whitefish. And she had brought Phoebe with her, probably by train. That much Jack knew. Phoebe was with Mrs. Dorothy now. But where was Maggie? *She has to be at her house*, thought Jack as he reviewed his newly acquired data. *Back to Park Avenue*, he concluded as he settled into Ida's blue Datsun once again.

This time when Jack pulled up in front of the house, he decided to pull over. Stop for a moment. Study the place. He noticed the shade in the front window had been drawn. He was sure that wasn't the case earlier. Still, no car in front. No other sign of Maggie or anyone else. It was a fairly large piece of property. More rural than a few blocks over on Second. Nice setting. An easy walk to town, but not in town. At one time, this place was probably home to chickens, a horse or two, maybe a cow. Built in the mid to late '70s would be Jack's guess. And on the back corner of the lot was a large barn. A man's dream. All kinds of stuff could be stored in there. A nightmare to everyone else, though. All kinds of hidden treasures and crap that would have to be discarded when the guy died.

I could just walk up to the door and knock, thought Jack. Why did that seem like such a bad idea? *Or I could leave.* Jack pulled out a quarter. *Heads I stay. Tails I leave.* He flipped it.

Chapter Forty-Two

Friday afternoon, 12:10 p.m.

Matt peered out the window from the upstairs bedroom and paused for a moment. Some guy sitting in a car across the street. He didn't look like a cop. Not at all. In fact, this guy looked rough and scrawny. Like a kid. Could be a cop, though. They were getting smarter like that. *Well, I'm getting smarter, too*, thought Matt as he closed the curtains and walked away from the window. This cop didn't look anything like the ones earlier. And a blue Datsun? *Pretty clever*, thought Matt. *What cop would drive a blue Datsun?*

They're not going to find anything here, including me, thought Matt, smiling. *Not me, not Maggie, nothing.* He'd learned long ago to be prepared and to expect the unexpected.

From the force of the blow, he figured he had a few more hours before Maggie would come to. And she'd behave regardless. She had no choice now. He'd made sure of that.

He went downstairs and tidied up a bit. No blood stains, so that was good. He straightened the two chairs in the living room and fluffed the pillows on the couch. Things needed to look normal in case the cops did get a search warrant. They probably would eventually. Back through the kitchen, out the back door, and quietly up the hill to his car. Nothing more he could do here for a while, so he decided to take a drive.

Chapter Forty-Three

Friday afternoon, 2 p.m.

Fix this, Maggie! her silenced scream demanded.

When her mom's radiation treatments had begun, Maggie had spent her afternoons picking every single four-leaf clover she could find. She'd pressed them carefully between two sheets of wax paper and ironed them, hoping to stockpile an abundance of good luck.

It would take her twice as long to walk home from school each day because she was consciously, carefully, avoiding every crack in the sidewalk.

And for breakfast? Every single morning, Lucky Charms. She had hated them. They actually made her want to gag. But she had endured. Because if eating them would help, it would be worth it.

She had needed all the luck she could squeeze out of the universe, and she had known it.

She hadn't told anyone she was doing all of this, of course. Not even her dad. If she had explained her attempts to increase her luck, to fix things, to change outcomes, it might have jinxed everything. So she had done it all quietly, thoughtfully, secretively, relentlessly.

Day after day, week after week, month after month, bite after bite.

None of it had mattered, though. None of it had helped. On that brilliantly sunny September morning, her mother had stopped breathing. The end.

Maggie had thrown away her vast collection of waxed-paper four-leaf clovers, stepped on every crack she came across, and torn up the last of her half-dozen boxes of Lucky Charms.

"Sometimes bad things happen to good people, Maggie." That's what her father had said. The school counselor had tried to console her with the most frustrating message of all. "Sometimes," she had said, "we can't fix things. We can't change things. We just have to accept them as they are."

So why do we try so hard? Maggie wondered. *Try harder, work longer, run faster. Isn't that what we're taught? You can do this. You can fix that.* If someone failed, it was because they hadn't tried hard enough. Or they obviously didn't want it badly enough.

As Maggie sat in the cold, dank cellar, tied and bound, these thoughts raced through her mind.

I wanted to save my mom, thought Maggie. *More than anything in the world. But I couldn't do it. I couldn't save her. I couldn't even help her.* As these thoughts ran through her head, she tried desperately to loosen the rope cutting into her wrists.

I couldn't help her. I couldn't fix her. And I can't fix Matt either. He is who he is, and he's done what he's done.

But I can help me. That's the one thing I can do.

Maggie wiggled her wrists back and forth, slowly loosening the grip they had on her. She could feel the rope cutting into her flesh, rubbing it raw. Faster, longer, harder. *I can fix this*, she repeated to herself. *I can. I have to.*

Chapter Forty-Four

Friday afternoon, 4 p.m.

Sitting outside in his car, Jack smiled as he looked at the coin he had pressed to the back of his hand. *Tails. That works for me. I didn't want to knock anyway. I'm not looking for trouble. I'm just looking for Maggie*, thought Jack as he slipped the quarter back into his pocket, started up the engine, and headed back to Mrs. Dorothy's.

The afternoon's light was starting to fade as he drove down the now familiar street. The children who had once littered the sidewalks on this surprisingly warm late-winter day were now making their way to their homes. Jack could almost smell the imaginary stews and big pots of chili that would be waiting for them. Through the windows, moments before the shades would be drawn, he could see the husbands, wives, and children all retreating into their houses after a long day. He could almost hear the excited chatter as everyone shared the highlights of the past eight hours.

As Jack pulled up in front of Mrs. Dorothy's, he was relieved to see he hadn't missed out entirely; he was still in time for hot chocolate on the front porch. *No signs of Maggie here yet either*, he thought as he stepped out of the car. This was as good a place as any to wait for her. Phoebe was here; Maggie soon would be too.

"Join us for a cup of hot chocolate, Jack?" asked Mrs. Dorothy. "Can't sit inside on a day like today."

"Don't mind if I do," he said, nodding politely as he reached out for his toasty warm mug. He noticed a heaping mound of fluffy white whipped cream on top. *Perfection*, he thought with a smile.

"And you may have a cookie too, Jack. But just one," said Phoebe as she passed the plate to him.

"Thank you, Phoebe. How was your afternoon? What have you been doing since I last saw you?" He'd always wanted to participate in the end-of-day chatter, a ritual that had never really been a part of his world.

Phoebe began a long list of all the things that had happened in Jack's absence. Two boys from her old kindergarten class walked by and said hello. The neighbor's dog got loose, and that was scary. But he wasn't as mean as he looked.

Jack grinned. This little taste of everyday normal was something he'd always longed for, without realizing it. At the end of his school day, he'd be greeted by three cookies. *Don't get me wrong*, he corrected himself, *those three cookies were probably more than I deserved most days. And Mum had to work hard to ensure I got those—plus the roof over my head and dinner. All that stuff. But to come home to chatter, and to have someone interested in what you'd been doing for the last six or so hours; it's hard to imagine the difference that could make in someone's life.*

"Did you take the dog back home? Or did he just wander off?" asked Jack.

"Oh, Mr. Kirby came and got him," Phoebe said.

"I see," Jack replied. "Maybe the dog just wanted one of these delicious cookies." As he finished up the last bite of his, he looked up and saw a big smile on Mrs. Dorothy's face. *She aims to please,* thought Jack.

Just then, a large white pickup slowly drove by. It pulled over as if to park in front of the house. Mrs. Dorothy stood up.

"Phoebe, your mom's here!" she sang out.

Jack's heart jumped a little. He was surprised by how nervous he was. It'd been maybe a week since he'd seen Maggie. Not even, he realized. Just three days. But it felt like longer. He stood and faced the street with a big grin on his face.

But the truck didn't stop. It slowed as if it would, but then it pulled out and drove away.

"Sorry, Phoebe. I thought it was your mom."

Not Maggie at all, thought Jack. From what he could see, it had been some tall, husky-looking man. An angry-looking man.

"Was that Daddy?" asked Phoebe. "Why didn't he stop, Mrs. Dorothy?"

"I'm not sure if that was your daddy, Phoebe. If it was your daddy, he would've stopped. So it must've been someone else. Your mom should be here soon, sweetie. Finish up your cookie. You've got a little more time to play left in the day." She smiled. "And if she isn't here before long, I'll fix you a nice big plate of dinner. You too, Jack."

Chapter Forty-Five

Friday afternoon, 4:15 p.m.

What the hell, thought Matt as he pulled up to Mrs. Dorothy's house. *Why is that cop here? That's the same damn cop who was parked outside my house just a few hours ago. Why the hell is he here? And with Phoebe, no less.*

Matt had driven over to pick up his daughter and bring her home. Where she belonged. Obviously, that wasn't going to happen. Not now anyway. As he slowed to a crawl, he studied Jack as best he could. Yep, same scruffy young punk-looking cop. *Well, he's not going to see me if I can help it*, thought Matt as he turned his face away from the house and started to drive down the street.

Another close call. Too many lately. *I must not have my shit together*, he concluded. *Tighten up your act, asshole*, he scolded himself. *This only works if you're in control. Nothing works if you're not.*

Okay, let's review. The cops are on to me. They've been to my house and now they're waiting for me at Mrs. Dorothy's. What are they looking for? Me, obviously. But what do they know? Has to be that broad who had Maggie's cell phone. The one back in Wolf Point. Roberta. Or Rebecca. Whatever her name was. Somehow they've tracked that mishap back to me. Couldn't have been the bullet, though. That gun isn't registered to me. I'm not that stupid. Must've been Maggie's cell phone. I shoulda gone back for it, I know. But again, I wiped it clean. My texts are gone. Why did that broad have Maggie's cell phone anyway? Were they friends? I would've known if they were friends. I know Maggie's friends. She wasn't one of them.

Matt drove to the end of the block and pulled over for a minute. Before heading home, he figured he'd better have an idea of what he was doing. What he needed to do next.

Hunters don't just go wandering into the woods, willy-nilly. No, they have a plan. They take what they need and they know where they're going. The successful ones, anyway. And Matt was a successful one. The proof of that? It was all over the walls of his house. Deer heads, wolves, even a bear, mounted and on display. These were his trophies. These were monuments to his refined ability to think, track, and trap.

What most people don't realize, thought Matt, *is that hunting isn't simply about the meat. If I wanted meat, I'd go buy meat. It's more like a sport. An opportunity to outsmart your enemy. And it doesn't just happen. No, it takes planning, calculating, precision. If it's executed correctly, the hunter walks away with a trophy, a monument to his ability to outsmart his opponent.* That was true with most of the sports Matt had participated in during high school. But there was something more that appealed to Matt about hunting. Whereas other sports offered trophies to the victors, only hunting allowed Matt to stuff and mount his actual opponents on the wall. Only hunting allowed him to create a shrine to himself, where clearly he was the master of his domain.

"Think. Think. Think," Matt said out loud as he knocked his palm against the side of his head. *You need to be smart about this,* he reminded himself. *You need to get Phoebe out of there. Not now, obviously, but as soon as possible. Or Mrs. Dorothy will start to worry. But in order to save Phoebe from the cop, you have to wait for the cop to leave.* A waiting game, he realized. *I am a hunter. I can wait. I'll go check on Maggie.*

Still being cautious, Matt drove his truck back up to his neighbor's house and parked it in their driveway. As he headed down to the barn, he noticed he was starting to cut a path through the overgrown vegetation. "Tracks," he said to himself. "That's the last thing I want to leave behind."

All quiet at the farm, he thought, as he went first to the house to get a good stiff shot of whiskey—to calm his nerves and give him fortitude. He walked upstairs. To Phoebe's room. He sat on the floor for a minute opposite the muraled wall. He studied it. He wasn't an artist; that was for sure. But it wasn't half bad. When Maggie was five months pregnant with Phoebe, he'd started it. Bought a few cans of paint, a collection of paint brushes, and some stencils. He'd spent a few hours every night, for four months straight, after Maggie went to sleep, creating this masterpiece. He couldn't carry the baby, or give birth to her, but this he could do. And for some reason, it seemed important to him. Here on the opposite wall was a scene straight from the forest. A deer peering her head out from behind a tree. A little fawn beside her. A mother bird perched on her nest, guarding her eggs. A few squirrels, two rabbits. All the forest animals he could think of he'd painted in such a way that they would be watching over his sleeping baby. Sitting here now, all those feelings of helplessness washed back over him. He didn't consider himself sentimental or superstitious, but he liked the idea of all these forest dwellers keeping watch over his Phoebe as she slept. Silly, he knew, but still. Somehow this felt necessary to him.

After a few moments, Matt stood, picked up his shot glass, and left the room, closing the door behind him. He walked back down to the kitchen where he rinsed out his shot glass with warm water before placing it in the dishwasher. Then he headed out the back door.

He lumbered to the barn, like a man twenty years his senior. He was killing time before going back to Mrs. Dorothy's to bring Phoebe home. A certain sadness hung over him. He couldn't even name it or identify it. Just a feeling he kept trying to shake off.

Once inside the barn, Matt stood there. Quietly. He looked around. There were saddles hanging from the beams above. Straw and hay all over the ground, just like in the barns he had grown up with. But those barns had horses. And chickens.

Suddenly, he heard a noise from down below. *It can't be Maggie*, he thought. *I secured her. She's not going anywhere.* But something was definitely going on down there. He walked over, and started to lift the heavy door. Halfway up, he heard the barn door behind him creak open.

Instantly, he dropped the floor door, creating an unexpected boom. That was one door he was always careful never to slam. Beneath it, his private world. A place he could go and always feel safe. Where he could really just be himself. He never would've put Maggie down there, but where else could he have kept her? The cops lurking around weren't helping any of this either.

Making sure the floor door was secure, Matt turned and headed toward the barn door. It was open. And he was sure he had closed it. He was always sure to close that door behind him. He reached under his belt and felt his gun. Yep. He walked to the door, slowly, surely. Probably the cops? Who else would it be? He opened the door and stood there. Turned his head to the left. Nothing. To the right. No one there either. He stood there for a moment, knowing the door didn't just open by itself. He took three steps out, looked some more. He took three steps back, landing him inside the barn again. He latched the door. Because that's what he did. He always latched that door. And he returned to the floor door. He looked down at it. *The only way to secure this one*, he thought, *is to make sure no one knows it's here*. He carefully covered it up with straw and dirt. He made sure it looked like it didn't exist.

Then Matt went back out the barn door, once again latched it behind him, and took a good look around. Still, no sign of anyone. But he knew someone had been here. And he suspected they'd be back.

Chapter Forty-Six

Friday afternoon, 4:15 p.m.

"How could Matt do this?" Maggie muttered as she finally wiggled her wrists free of the ropes. Tight. Painfully tight. *But not as tight as he could've made them*, she thought. *Maybe he didn't really want to hurt me. Maybe this—all of this—was just his way of asserting his power over me. A reclaiming of property that he considered rightfully his.*

Maggie stood for a moment and lifted her right hand to the throbbing knot on her head. It felt hot to the touch. She gently massaged it to help ease some of the pain. She felt moisture. She didn't need to look to know it was blood.

Maybe he didn't want to hurt you? Right, Maggie, she corrected herself. *I'm thinking maybe he did. Maggie, Maggie, Maggie*, she scolded herself over and over. *You have a gift for seeing people as you want them to be. And this is no gift. Dad was right. It doesn't matter what they say. It matters what they do.*

That was the thing about Matt, she admitted. He had always seemed to know what to say. She had been at a point in her life when she'd lost everything. Her mom to cancer. Her dad to a heart attack. And then there was Matt. Reassuring, strong, promising to be there for her. He had offered her a family of her own. Everything she'd always dreamed of.

She thought back to the moment when they had said goodnight on their second date.

"Maggie," he said softly, "I've never felt this way about any one before."

He reached out and held her hand.

"I like you too, Matt," she shyly replied.

"No, I really mean it. From the moment I first saw you, I knew you were the one."

Her heart raced. *How could anyone know anything with such certainty?* she wondered.

"I'm going to marry you, Maggie," he said.

Unable to find words, she giggled girlishly.

As they walked together up to her door that night, he stopped and turned to face her.

"Will you go out with me again?" he asked.

"Yes, I would love to," she said.

"Okay, good. I'll pick you up tomorrow at seven." He grinned victoriously.

"We just went out last night and tonight," she said.

"I know." He smiled as he kissed her softly on the check. As he started to make his way down the stairs, he stopped, turned, and shouted, "I'm going to ask you out every night until you say you want to marry me too, Maggie!"

Maggie closed the door behind her and stood there for a few minutes. Just two dates. Everything was happening so quickly. But she wasn't complaining. "Until you say you want to marry me too, Maggie," she repeated to herself.

When she was with Matt, she didn't feel lost. Or alone. Or sad. She just felt magic.

But fairytale magic fades. And theirs had seemed to fade quickly. As soon as he was successful in his quest, once again settled into a routine, things changed.

"Can't you shut that baby up!" he'd scream if Phoebe were crying. Maggie would cradle Phoebe gently, bundle her up, and walk her around the yard to settle her down.

"Shh. Shh. Shh," she'd coo. "It'll be okay, sweet baby. Your dad, he's just a little upset. He'll be okay too."

Something, anything, would set him off. And sometimes nothing was required. When Maggie was young, she remembered visiting Yellowstone with her dad. And her favorite part, aside from the buffalo, was Old Faithful. She'd never seen a geyser before and was quite impressed with how it would periodically erupt at almost perfect intervals. Beneath the surface, her dad explained, pressure would build, and build, and build, until it had to be released. And then, like clockwork, it would spew forth jets of water and steam, high into the air. Afterwards, it would go quiet again. As Maggie imagined, Old Faithful probably felt pretty good at that moment, having let off all that steam. But she also knew that beneath the surface, the pressure was already starting to build, preparing for the next eruption.

To Maggie, Matt was simply Old Faithful. All would seem fine, but beneath the surface, she could almost sense the pressure building. And then it would spew. It was because Phoebe was crying. Or a car in front of him was going too slowly. Maybe Maggie wasn't dressed appropriately. It didn't really seem to matter. When the pressure built, it had to be released.

How many times had this happened in the past five years? Maggie couldn't say. She did know it had been escalating. The angry words were starting to morph into angry gestures. And his anger toward her had started to drift toward Phoebe.

How long have I been here, tied up like this? Maggie couldn't be sure. And where was "here"? She didn't have an answer for that either. *I've got to go get Phoebe. Before Matt does.*

Suddenly, she heard noises above her. Something slammed shut. A door, maybe? Not just any door, but the clanking, heavy sound of wood on wood. Another boom right above her. Her eyes followed a set of old wooden steps going up to the ceiling. There, at the top, was an old wooden door with rusty wrought-iron hinges. *I'm in a basement*, she concluded. She reached down and touched the ground. *Yep, dirt. Makes sense.*

A basement where, though? And how do I get out of here? From what Maggie could see, there was a chair, the chair she'd been tied to, in the center of the room. A dirt floor. No windows. One other door toward the back. And the only other way out—up.

The sole light was an exposed bulb dangling above her, illuminating the room and casting shadows on the wall in front of her. The far wall was lined with old cabinets, antique white cabinets with paint chipping off the corners. Maggie recognized them immediately. They were the old ones from her kitchen when they had remodeled a few years ago. She walked over, touched the handle, and nodded her head definitively. She opened one of the cabinet doors and stepped back suddenly. Inside were jars and jars of all sizes. Filled with liquid. Some had small beetles floating in them. A few ladybugs. Some bees and wasps. In the second cabinet, no jars, but tiny animals seemingly frozen. A cute little mouse standing on its hind legs, as if begging for food. *Maybe it was begging for life*, she thought sadly. Above it to the right was a small bird in flight, with wings wide open, suspended perhaps by a transparent wire? She wasn't sure.

And the final cabinet? She hesitated for a moment. She slowly opened the door, and inside, dead center, an oversized glass jar filled with a larger furry creature. Maggie reached her hand into the cabinet and slowly rotated the jar. "Oh my God!" she squealed. Inside this jar was Spunky, Phoebe's first kitten. Her tiny little black face smashed up against the inside of the glass. Maggie's heart dropped. Spunky had gone missing. They'd spent so many days searching for her, from dawn until dusk, swinging flashlights through the trees, calling her name, crying. Had she been here, trapped in this jar, the entire time? How did she get here? Did Matt do this? To Phoebe's Spunky? Why? *Another question that probably doesn't need an answer,* thought Maggie, as she wrapped her arms around her stomach as if to hold it in place.

Being hit with a gun upside her head was nothing compared to what she was feeling at this moment. Her head was spinning, swirling, as if it were going to explode. She brought her hands up from her stomach and grabbed her head tightly.

"Spunky. Oh my god, Spunky. I am so, so sorry." She started to sob. She picked up the jar and cradled it in her arms.

It's one thing to run from something you don't want to see. *If I run fast enough,* thought Maggie, *it will be as if I never saw it. So it doesn't exist.* But this wasn't one of those times. Sometimes you can't unsee what you've seen. And you can't undo what's been done. *Run, Maggie. Run!* she told herself as she slammed the cabinet door loudly. Too loudly.

She heard more noises upstairs, this time closer. Someone was coming. Someone was right over her head.

Chapter Forty-Seven

Friday afternoon, 4:30 p.m.

"Are you making franks and beans for dinner, Mrs. Dorothy? Those are my favorites," said Phoebe, who was apparently getting a bit hungry.

"Do you like frank and beans, Jack?" Phoebe looked directly at Jack, who was sitting across from her on the porch.

"I do, Ms. Phoebe. I do!" he said. On the outside, Jack was all in, deeply engrossed in their conversation about dinner. But inside, his mind was spinning. *I don't much care for the looks of that guy*, he thought, *as he tried hard to concentrate on what Phoebe was saying.* He'd seen a lot of angry men in prison. Explosive men. And that guy in the old white Chevy truck could've been one of them.

"Mrs. Dorothy," said Jack, "I need to run to town for a moment. Gotta pick something up at the store. Can I get you anything?" he asked.

"Can I go with you, Jack?" asked Phoebe, pleading.

"Not this time, Phoebe. But I won't be long. I'll bring you back something. How's that?" he offered as a consolation prize.

Phoebe smiled. Nothing better than the anticipation of an unknown prize.

"You know, Jack, I could use half a gallon of milk, if you go to a grocery store."

"Okay, you got it. A surprise for Phoebe and milk for Dorothy," he replied as he stood up and shook each of his legs as if to straighten them out. "Back in a flash," he said as he practically skipped down the steps. One thing Jack had never mastered—sitting still. He'd much rather be running an errand or just plain running than sitting still.

The store can wait, he thought as he drove straight to Maggie's. Jack could feel it; something wasn't right. Maggie was in some kind of trouble. As he pulled up to the house, there was no white truck in the driveway. No tracks in the driveway either. "I'll circle the block. It has to be here somewhere. Because he has to be here. I just know it."

Jack drove around the block. It wasn't really a block. The street meandered up a hill, then split to the right and to the left, the right going straight up the hill. Jack went left. Nothing. "Figures," he said out loud. "I always have to go the wrong way first." He backtracked to the right. Sure enough, there was the white truck up on the hill, in a driveway. It was the right one. Definitely. It had the same busted-out taillight and missing license plate. Jack parked a few houses down and wandered over. From the front of the house, he could look down on what had to be Maggie's property. A big barn. Lots of trees. From up here, you had a pretty good shot at what was below, even the street.

The way down was easy enough too. A narrow path ran between this yard and the next. At the back of the property, a newly formed path seemed to meander down the hill, through the trees. Jack traversed it slowly, cautiously. He felt a bit empty-handed and unprotected. No gun or knife. Nothing. But here he was, heading into the unknown.

Maybe he didn't even need a gun. Or a knife. Maybe he didn't have to rescue her. Maybe he didn't have to have the answers. Maybe, maybe this time, he just needed to show up. For his own peace of mind.

It felt like there had been too many times in his life when he hadn't done anything. Or wasn't in the right state of mind to do anything. So he did nothing.

He wasn't proud of who he was. He ran from everything. He drank too much. Everything was a party, an escape, a big joke. And none of it was his responsibility.

The one thing Jack had learned these past few years was he always had a choice. He could be that guy, the guy who no one could count on. Or he could be the kind of friend he'd want to have. The one you could count on. And be proud of.

As he approached the barn, he slowed down, listened. Tried to find out as much as he could before going in. There was no sight or sound of Maggie.

Jack walked around the outside of the barn, trying to figure out what he was up against. There were no windows, just a large wooden door with rusty old hinges. *No way I can quietly open that sucker*, he thought. But he was going to have to go in, as quietly as he possibly could. What other choice did he have?

Jack walked back to the barn door and stood there for a moment. He inhaled deeply and placed both of his hands on the long wooden bar that latched the door in place. Slowly, he lifted it, as quietly as he could. He moved the barn door open just a few inches, just enough to set the wooden bar back down. It was unlatched. Opened. He slowly pushed the door just a tiny bit, waiting for a reaction from within. Nothing. He stood there for another moment, waiting for noise. He pushed the door open another inch. Slowly. Quietly.

He waited.

Another inch.

This time, he stopped abruptly. From inside the barn, he heard what sounded like a heavy thud, a large wooden something being dropped.

Jack left the door partly open and started to retreat. He stepped away, back toward the path. He tucked in behind a cluster of trees, the type of trees that offer protection from peering eyes or angry men with axes. He waited. Within seconds, the barn door swung wide open and out stepped that angry man. The angry man whipped his head from side to side, casing his surroundings. *That kind of anger wasn't anger*, thought Jack as he watched Matt madly searching for someone to release his fury on. *Anger was rational. Specific. This was rage.* In Jack's experience, there was no creature more terrifying than a man filled with this kind of rage.

Jack now knew Maggie was in there and in danger. That much was clear. What to do about it, he wasn't sure yet. But he knew he had to figure it out.

Chapter Forty-Eight

Friday afternoon, 4:30 p.m.

The footsteps grew louder until they were right over Maggie's head. Then suddenly, the floor door above her swung wide open. It had to be Matt. Quickly, Maggie moved to the back of the room and crouched on the floor. As if this would hide her. And just as suddenly, the floor door slammed shut again. She knew it wouldn't be long before he returned.

First thought that came to mind: *Is there another way out? Possibly out this back door.* Why was it padlocked? *Why,* she wondered, *would anyone padlock a door in a room that no one knew existed? Where would I hide the key if I were Matt?* She reached above the door, and sure enough, there was the key. She slipped it into the lock and turned it clockwise. It sprung open. She removed the lock, opened the door, and entered the room one step at a time, taking a few seconds between each carefully planted step.

Inside, to the left, more cabinets and a countertop. A knife, syringes, bottles, jars. Weird-looking stuff. *Am I in a laboratory?* she wondered as she picked up one of the small bottles and studied it.

Pentobarbital. Why? she wondered as she tucked it carefully into her front jeans pocket. Restraints of some sort were hanging off the side of the counter. What was this room?

On the other side of the room was an alcove, partitioned off with a pale blue curtain, a curtain certainly out of place in this sterile laboratory. *An old one from our dining room?* she wondered? *Had to be.* She walked over, and stood there for a moment. *Do I dare?* she wondered. Honestly, she could turn around now, go up the stairs, and get the hell out of here. She could go get Phoebe and leave this place forever. *Run!* a voice inside said. But then another voice quietly whispered, *Stay, Maggie. Stay.*

She was in too far, too deep. She had to see what else was here. That part of her brain that had to know wouldn't let her walk away. Not now.

"If you run away," her dad would say, "it doesn't change what you've run from. That thing will always be there. You either face it now, or you carry it with you forever."

"That doesn't make any sense, Dad," she would answer. "You get away from something by running away from something."

"The only way to get away from something, Maggie, is to face it."

As a child, this advice never made much sense to Maggie. If you don't like something, run. If something hurts too much, don't think about it. If you don't like what someone's doing, turn your head. To some degree, this had served her well. Up to a point. But now, she found herself married to a man who was capable of things she couldn't even comprehend. And she'd spent years pretending it wasn't so.

"Okay, Dad. I won't run," she said out loud as the pulled back the curtain.

There, lying in a bed, was a woman Maggie had never seen before. She was beautiful, peaceful. Auburn hair draped softly around her face. She couldn't be too much older than Maggie. Maybe mid-thirties? Her skin was practically flawless. She was lying motionless, so still. Maggie was surprised that all the noise, the slamming cabinets, the thunderous wood door dropping, hadn't woken her. Maggie moved a step closer.

"Excuse me," she said softly.

No response.

"Excuse me, miss," she said again.

Nothing.

She reached out and touched the woman delicately on the shoulder. Still no response. Maggie realized this woman couldn't feel the touch through her thick flannel shirt. Maggie reached out again and placed the palm of her hand on this woman's hand. Maggie jerked her hand back instantly. *This woman*, Maggie thought, *this woman is cold. Oh my God.... This woman is dead!*

Okay, now I run, Dad. Maggie screamed as she ran out of the room as fast as she could. *Where the hell am I? What is this house of horrors? Who is this dead woman? And why am I here?* She hurried up the stairs and managed to push the door wide open. Suddenly, she found herself in the barn. Her barn. She had been here the entire time. How could she have never known about this hidden basement? Maggie sighed deeply. How many times had Phoebe come to the barn, looking for her dad? How many hours each day did she play out here?

Maggie dropped the door back to the ground, bolted to the barn door, and ran out as fast as she could. It wasn't until she was well into the trees that she bent over and threw up all over the ground.

Chapter Forty-Nine

Friday afternoon, 5:15 p.m.

Jack slithered back up to his car, crawled inside, and waited. He sensed that angry man was probably too rattled to sit still now. He'd either try to bait Jack to come back, or he'd go get Phoebe to bring her home. Jack just had to wait to see which one he'd choose.

Sure enough, within the hour, Jack saw the old white Chevy truck back up and head out. *Okay, this is my chance*, thought Jack. *Probably my only chance.* As soon as the truck cleared the bottom of the hill, Jack knew he had at most forty minutes, but as little as ten. Depending on how social angry man was feeling. And Jack was guessing he wasn't feeling social at all. He couldn't quite picture this angry man sitting on Mrs. Dorothy's porch, sipping tea and discussing the weather or politics. Not today, anyway—not right after having his territory invaded. Jack jogged down the hill and stood momentarily in front of the large wooden barn door. "Okay, here goes," he said as he lifted the latch and cautiously entered the barn.

"Maggie?" he called out hopefully. No answer. He wasn't really expecting one. He surveyed the room carefully. *Looks like a barn, complete with saddles and tacking, horse blankets, hay—all of it. But somewhere in here, there's something worth protecting.* Jack started walking from one corner to the next, moving the blankets that hung on the walls, kicking the hay on the ground, looking for secret trap doors or hidden rooms. *This place reminds me of Grandpa Kline's, built back when everyone had a trap door, hidden room, or a bomb shelter. Where they'd store enough canned goods to survive a nuclear blast. What a strange time to be alive,* thought Jack as he kicked one little cluster of hay and found just what he was looking for. There, directly in front of him on the ground, was an old wooden door. It was set in an indentation just slightly below the surface of the ground, just enough so that the door itself would fill it perfectly. The handle lay flat. And with a little dirt and hay kicked on top, no one would ever know. Jack pulled the handle and slowly lifted the heavy door.

"Maggie?" he called again. No answer. Down he went, step by step, slowly. It was a small room, with a low ceiling and dirt floors. In the center was a wooden chair with a rope or two at its foot. Jack walked over and picked up the rope. A piece of cloth fell to the ground. *A gag for a mouth?* he wondered. It had teeth marks in it.

"Maggie," he called again, this time with more empathy and perhaps some resignation in his voice. He was guessing these restraints had been hers. "Oh, Maggie," he sighed. "How did a nice girl like you end up in a place like this?" Out of the corner of his eye, he noticed the row of cabinets and wandered over to them. Without hesitation, he quickly opened the doors. *No sense prolonging this,* he thought. *Let's see what's behind door number one, door number two, and door number three.* Jars filled with dead animals. Bugs, mice, even a cat. For some reason, Jack wasn't surprised. He did a 180 and suddenly saw the other door. *Hidden door within a hidden room. Not liking this at all,* thought Jack as he walked toward the door. He had no idea what he was going to find, but he was pretty sure it wasn't going to be good. For anyone.

Before going any farther, he stopped. *You know what I could use,* he thought. *A good, stiff drink. Just one. Just enough to calm my nerves.* But deep down, Jack knew there was no such thing as just one drink. One would lead to two, and two would lead to another blackout drunk, passed out, on the side of the road. No, the luxury of just one drink was no longer Jack's. Was never Jack's actually. He breathed in slowly, deeply. There'd be no possible way he could find Maggie. Or help her. Or himself. Or anyone. *No, you're just afraid,* he told himself, *and you want to run. I get it. Well, guess what? We don't run from our fears. Not anymore. And we help friends. No matter what.*

"Ready?" he asked himself as he pulled back the curtain and took two steps back. "Okay, this isn't good. Not good at all," he said out loud as he looked at the perfectly preserved body of a woman, He didn't have to poke or prod her to know she wasn't going to wake up. She'd already seen her final sunrise. And he didn't need to see anything else.

Okay, that's enough for me, thought Jack as he backed out of the room. *I still haven't found Maggie. And I'm kind of grateful for that at the moment. Maybe, just maybe, she got away. I'll go find her. She's got to be heading back to Phoebe.*

Just as Jack was moving toward the stairs, the floor door above him slammed shut with a loud boom. Jack could hear a heavy object being dragged across the floor, then pushed on top of the door above him. *Shit! Guess I miscalculated angry man. Gone five minutes maybe? He's even more unsocial than I anticipated. Or maybe he didn't even go to Dorothy's.*

Well, thank God I have a phone, thought Jack as he pulled it out of this pocket. No service.

This isn't going according to plan, he thought as he sat down in the chair in the center of the room.

Chapter Fifty

Friday afternoon, 5:15 p.m.

Maggie managed to get back to Mrs. Dorothy's in record time.

"Mom!" yelled Phoebe, running down the front steps to greet her. "Mommie!"

"Hey, Phoebe!" called out Maggie. She picked her up and held her so tightly that Phoebe started to complain.

"Mom, you're hurting me!"

"I'm sorry. I'm just so happy to see you."

"Did you see Dad? I saw him. Mrs. Dorothy said I didn't, but I did. Jack thought it was him too. And Jack doesn't even know him."

"Jack?" asked Maggie, confused and trying hard to follow Phoebe's train of thought. "Why was Jack here?"

"I don't know. He just came by," said Phoebe.

Maggie looked at her incredulously. She then turned to look at Mrs. Dorothy for validation or clarification. Mrs. Dorothy shook her head up and down to signify, *Yes, Phoebe's right.*

"Where did he go?" asked Maggie.

"To the store. To get me a present," said Phoebe.

Maggie again looked at Mrs. Dorothy and once again received a nod.

Jack wouldn't have gone to the house, would he? Maggie wondered. Oh, this couldn't be good. If he had come to help her, he had no idea what he was walking into. He had no clue who Matt really was. She hadn't even known who Matt truly was or what he was capable of. Until now. *It's my mess,* she thought. *And it just keeps getting bigger. So much for that idea of picking up Phoebe and running away.*

"Mrs. Dorothy," Maggie said, "can I talk to you for a minute? In the kitchen?"

Mrs. Dorothy nodded once again and led the way into the house.

"Back in one minute, Phoebe," promised Maggie as she followed Mrs. Dorothy inside.

Mrs. Dorothy could see that, clearly, Maggie was rattled. Mrs. Dorothy led her into the kitchen and poured her a shot of peppermint schnapps. Maggie never drank, but today, it turns out, she did.

"Thank you," she said as she tipped it back quickly. Mrs. Dorothy filled it back up. She wasn't sure what was going on, but she was guessing a drink would make it a bit better. "I just need a minute," said Maggie.

"You sit here, dear. I'll leave this with you," she said as she set the bottle down in front of Maggie. "We can talk more later if you want…."

"Wait, what do you know about this?" Maggie reached into her front pocket and pulled out the small bottle of pentobarbital that she had taken from the barn.

"Pentobarbital? That'll knock a horse out. What are you doing with this?"

"I found it at home."

"Careful. One jab of that to the neck and the person is out. For hours."

"Here?" Maggie pointed to a particular vein in her neck.

"Yeah, there. What are you up to, Maggie?" asked Mrs. Dorothy without really wanting to know the answer.

"Nothing." Maggie shook her head.

"Okay, I'll go sit with Phoebe out on the front porch. Make sure she's okay. You be careful, Maggie," said Mrs. Dorothy as she shuffled down the hall and out onto the porch.

Chapter Fifty-One

Friday afternoon, 5:45 p.m.

Matt laughed smugly as he slid the old iron safe on top of the trap door. *Little fucker*, he thought. *Who the hell does he think he is? I knew he'd be back. I knew he was watching me. And now I've trapped him like a damn fly.*

Matt smiled. *What's one less cop? If you snag one, though, a whole bunch more going to be buzzing around soon. Better don't dilly dally*, he thought as he headed toward his truck. This time, he'd parked it out front. No need to hide from this particular cop anymore. And now, the coast was clear to go get Phoebe. Within a matter of minutes, he was pulling up in front of Mrs. Dorothy's. And there on the porch was just who he wanted to see. Little Phoebe.

"Daddy. Hi, Daddy!" called Phoebe.

"Hello, stranger," hollered Mrs. Dorothy as she waved to Matt. "Did you drive by earlier? Phoebe was sure that was you, but I said no, if that was your daddy, he would've stopped. Was that you?"

He hardly heard a word she said. He smiled at Phoebe.

"Hey, baby, come here. Give me a hug."

Phoebe looked over at Mrs. Dorothy, then walked slowly over to Matt. He picked her up effortlessly and gave her a big bear hug.

"Where have you been? I've been missing my little Pheebs," said Matt.

"Why didn't you come with us?" she asked as she sat somewhat rigidly on his lap.

"Your mom, she didn't invite me."

Phoebe didn't say anything for a moment. Her little eyes were darting back and forth as if she were trying hard to remember if he was telling the truth.

"Did you do something bad?" she finally asked. She twirled the string from her hoodie round and round her finger.

"No, she just got mad at me."

After a few moments of thoughtful quiet, Phoebe softly said, "You scared me, Daddy. You were yelling." She didn't look at him when she said this.

His body stiffened. Of course he had been yelling. He'd been upset. And he'd had every right to be. But right now, he needed to stay calm, to stay in control.

Phoebe stopped playing with the string. She tensed a little too.

"It's okay, baby. Nobody's mad now," he said.

She softened a little.

"Do you know Jack? I like Jack," she said.

"Jack? Who's Jack?"

"Mom's friend. He came with us on the train," said Phoebe, hesitant once again.

"Jack?" Matt stood up, almost knocking Phoebe to the ground.

"Daddddd," pleaded Phoebe.

Mrs. Dorothy stood up from her end of the porch and started to make her way over.

"Who the hell is Jack?" demanded Matt.

"He was just here, Daddy," Phoebe started to answer before she realized that now was one of those times she just needed to keep her mouth shut.

Mrs. Dorothy instinctively moved behind Phoebe and skirted her inside the house.

"Got some cookies waiting for you in there, sweetie. Go!" she commanded. She shoved Phoebe in the door. Phoebe didn't hesitate. She went. Quickly.

Matt started to follow, but Mrs. Dorothy stood in the way, as if by accident.

"Out of my way," said Matt.

Mrs. Dorothy took two steps back, pulled her cell phone out of her apron pocket, and said, "You back up, buddy, or I'm calling the police."

Matt stopped. If there was anyone he thought he could easily intimidate, it would've been Mrs. Dorothy. She was the picture of a sweet, quiet, adoring grandmother. Soft and loving. Spent her entire life taking care of others.

"Okay, just take it easy. No need to call the police," he said as he took one step back. He never would've pegged her for a woman to be reckoned with. But she was angry. And she wasn't about to budge. Besides, he needed to pick his battles carefully now. The last thing he wanted was more police showing up. He almost laughed. Stopped by a grandma. *She has no clue who she's up against*, thought Matt. *Just as well. I need to diffuse. Collect my thoughts, check on Maggie. And her dear friend Jack.* He felt his anger starting to rise instantly, uncontrollably. Phoebe would just have to wait a bit longer, concluded Matt as he stepped off the porch and made his way to his car.

Chapter Fifty-Two

Friday evening, 6:30 p.m.

Maggie sat at the kitchen table, holding Phoebe, who was shaking.

"Why was daddy so angry at me?" asked Phoebe.

Maggie wiped Phoebe's tears with the end of her sleeve. "It's not your fault, Phoebe. You didn't do anything wrong." She held her tightly and stroked the back of her hair.

Mrs. Dorothy entered the room, holding her cell phone up as if it were the largest machine gun in the world. "He's gone," she said proudly.

"I've got to go help Jack. I think he's in trouble," said Maggie. "I promise you, Phoebe, I will be back to get you. Soon. Very soon. You stay here just a bit longer with Mrs. Dorothy, okay?"

Mrs. Dorothy nodded. "I got her. Maggie, you want me to really call the police?"

"Not yet. But thanks." Maggie realized Phoebe was in the best place she could be at this moment. And that's what mattered most. But now she had to get to Jack before Matt did. She gave Mrs. Dorothy a quick hug, and out the back door she ran.

Within minutes, Maggie was at the back of her house, just steps from the barn door. She could see Matt's white truck parked proudly out front. *Hopefully*, thought Maggie, *he's in the house. Having a drink, or a smoke, or a chew. Something to calm him down.* She knew him well enough to know this was not the time you'd want to run into Matthew McCauley. The old geyser would be about ready to blow.

Maggie ran to the barn, opened the door, and quietly closed it behind her. She scanned the room. No sign of Matt. No sign of Jack, either. Which didn't mean he wasn't there. She tiptoed to the floor door and started to shove the old iron safe away from the top of it. It was heavier than she'd imagined, but she was relentless. Finally, it budged. She lifted the door and looked down. There was Jack, looking up. She pointed her index finger to her lips. "Shh." He nodded. She smiled. She stepped down the ladder as fast as she could and gave him a quick hug.

"I'm guessing he's in the house. We don't have long," she whispered. He nodded again.

"Can you go up and make sure he doesn't come down?" she asked. "I need a minute. There's something I need to do."

"Yeah, I can do that," he replied. "But just for a minute. This guy is crazy."

Jack went up the stairs and closed the floor door quietly behind him. Maggie walked over to the back door in the basement and entered slowly. She opened the cabinet filled with syringes, bottles, and jars. She studied them intently. She picked up one of the syringes and pulled the bottle from her pocket. She inserted the needle into the jar, pulled it out, and then set it down carefully on the counter. She closed the cabinets.

She stood at the end of the bed where the dead lady lay. She stroked her hair as if to soothe her.

And sure enough, within minutes, the wooden door above opened. It didn't slam. Maggie heard someone slowly lumbering down the steps, someone not in a hurry, someone perhaps at the end of a long journey, she imagined. She stood still, waiting, Suddenly, the curtain was pulled back dramatically, and there stood Matt.

"Maggie!" he said surprised. "I wasn't expecting you."

"Who were you expecting?" she asked.

Maggie noticed Matt looking at her and then looking at the dead woman in front of her. He looked embarrassed.

"Maggie." He paused. "Lisa," he added, as if introducing the two of them to each other.

Maggie just stared incredulously at him.

After a moment, Matt took a step forward.

"I can explain," he said, much like a man caught with another woman might try to tell his wife it really wasn't what it looked like.

"Your ex?" asked Maggie. She shook her head from side to side, in disgust.

"Maggie," he said, a guttural tone to his voice, "this never woulda happened," he started to explain, attempting to deflect blame onto her. She felt it coming.

She stood quietly. Expectantly. If she'd learned anything these past six years, it was you don't rock the boat. You don't upset Matt. The unspoken rule in the house. Because once you do, you don't know what's going to happen.

But she couldn't help it. She shook her head from side to side, in undeniable disgust. There was no hiding her emotions now. There was no holding back.

"It's your fault, Maggie. I never would…" he continued.

Maggie started to shake her head rapidly from one side to the other, with the enthusiasm of a defiant child.

"Maggie," he scolded. He took another step forward.

"No. No. No. No!" she said firmly. He stopped as a hunter approaching a rabid animal might. Uncertain and cautious. He looked surprised.

She took a deep breath. In and out. She started slowly. "It's not my fault, Matt. None of this."

"Maggie, if you hadn't…"

"Hadn't what, Matt?" She pointed to the dead woman in front of her. "No, you can't put this one on me. Never saw her before.

I'm guessing she's been here longer than I've been in your life. Am I right, Matt?"

"If you hadn't," he started again.

"Hadn't what, Matt?" she repeated. She looked him directly in the eyes. She wasn't afraid. This was something new. She wasn't afraid. And that was making Matt nervous.

"You can't change a man who doesn't want to change," she said, to herself mostly. "And you can't reason with insanity."

She shook her head slowly and watched as the man she had married started once again to fill with rage. She could almost see it, starting at his feet, she imagined. Building, expanding, moving upward. Consuming him. Blinding him. True to form, within seconds, he lunged at her. This time, though, she was ready. She stood her ground. She didn't budge. She didn't run. As his six-three frame torpedoed into hers, she grabbed the needle, jabbed it firmly into his neck, and pushed with every ounce of self-preservation she had left.

"This has to stop, Matt," she whispered in his ear as his body froze in shock, stunned that Maggie could do such a thing. His face turned to the counter where the tiny bottle of pentobarbital stood, center stage. His eyes, Maggie noted, were racing frantically, darting from one side of the room to the other, perhaps as he was recalling the countless animals he had rendered unconscious with the exact same drug.

"What have you done, Maggie?" Matt demanded. "What have you done?"

Maggie figured the drug would take a minute or two to kick in. All she had to do now was keep him talking and distracted for just a moment longer.

"You were going to hurt me, Matt."

"I wouldn't hurt you, Maggie. I love you."

Maggie looked over at the corpse on the table.

"Is that what you said to her, too?"

"That was different, Maggie. That was all her fault."

She felt his anger starting to rise again. She paused for a moment. Unable to stop herself, she cautiously continued.

"And Rebecca. What about Rebecca?"

"That woman with your cell phone? In Wolf Point?"

"Yes, that woman."

Matt spoke slowly, as if trying to find the words. "Do you know what she said to me?" he asked. "Do you have any idea what she said to me? What she said to me. You don't know. She had it coming, Maggie."

"So you did shoot her? You did that?"

Before Matt could answer, his body slowly slumped and dropped to the ground.

She stood there, looking at a lifeless version of Matt lying in a clump on the ground. She stepped away from his body and seemed to take it all in—what had just happened and everything that had preceded it.

What would her dad say at this moment? None of his little sayings came to mind. *If you blame everyone else for your problems*, she reasoned, *then there's nothing you can do to change your circumstances. It's all his fault, or her fault, or their fault. Let's see; how would Dad put this? If you blame someone else for your problems, then they'll always be your problems.* Maggie smiled. "Now I'm starting to sound like my dad," she whispered with a smile.

Maggie hadn't heard Jack approaching, but there he was, standing on the other side of the curtain. He looked at Matt's body and then up to Maggie's face. Then his eyes went to the dead woman who lay peacefully between them.

"Could've been you, Maggie," he said.

"I know. I'm guessing this is his ex. I never saw pictures of her. Never knew she was here the whole time. Why?" she asked.

Jack walked over and hugged Maggie.

"She left work one day and never came back, Maggie. And no one went looking for her."

"Oh my God; that's so sad," said Maggie.

"He'd told someone that she'd gone to visit her sick mom or something like that. And it all stopped there," said Jack.

"So sad," Maggie repeated, realizing she'd left work one day, just the other day, without a word. And that probably no one would have come looking. "Could've been me," she whispered thoughtfully.

Maggie touched the woman's face softly. "I'm so sorry," as if the woman could hear. *To vanish and not be missed*, thought Maggie, *would be more tragic than anything else I could imagine.* She shuddered.

"Let's clean this up and get out of here," said Jack. He started to drag Matt's body from the ground up to the bed where the dead lady was lying. Maggie got on the other side, and together, they lifted him.

"Okay, let's go," said Maggie as the two of them headed out of the room and up the stairs to daylight.

At the top of the stairs, they shut the door behind them. They carefully pushed the hay and dirt back on top. As they were heading out the door, Jack stopped. He walked back over to where the hidden door was. He bent down and pushed the old iron safe back over the floor door. Maggie looked on inquisitively.

"He prefers it this way," said Jack.

They both knew they could leave him there, where he'd wake a few hours later, only to realize he was trapped in a dungeon of his own making. Trapped, alone—with no one looking for him. *What a way to die*, thought Maggie. *Unnoticed. Forgotten. The irony of it all.*

Jack and Maggie walked slowly back to Mrs. Dorothy's. On the way, Maggie said, "That poor woman. How long do you suppose she was down there?"

"No way to know. With embalming, could've been forever," Jack replied.

"Years maybe? Me and Phoebe in the house, and her in the basement."

"Better in the house than in the basement with her," said Jack. He reached out and held her hand as they walked.

"He murdered her," Maggie said. "And I'm pretty sure he's responsible for your friend's death too."

"Yeah, I really don't get that. What's the connection? I've been trying to figure all of that out," said Jack.

Maggie got quiet. "Oh, Jack, I'm partly to blame for that. Really. I am so sorry."

"What?" asked Jack.

"On the train. He kept texting my phone, endless texts. 'Where the hell are you?' 'I'm talking to you, bitch.' Over and over. It was early morning. I was exhausted. Done. You know, I could've just shut my phone off, but that never seems right. Doesn't feel responsible. Rebecca's bag was right there, in the aisle. Wide open. Seemed like the perfect solution. I figured she'd find it and toss it. Or he'd track it and end up with nothing. A wild goose chase. But it would keep him from hounding me. I didn't think about what could happen to her. Never would've thought any of this was possible. Didn't know what he was capable of…." Her voice trailed off.

"You couldn't have known, Maggie. That's really not on you." He squeezed her hand tighter as they reached Mrs. Dorothy's house.

"Mom! Jack!" called Phoebe when she saw them walking up the front porch.

Maggie picked up Phoebe and twirled her around three times. Phoebe laughed.

"I think everything's okay now," Maggie said to Mrs. Dorothy. "Thank you. Thank you for everything. Thank you for having our backs."

"Anytime, Maggie. You and Phoebe always have a place here. And there's a plot in the backyard if you need that too," she said, winking at Maggie.

Maggie gave her a big hug and thought, *Oh, Mrs. Dorothy, if you only knew!* Then she turned to Phoebe. "We'd better get going Phoebe. We've got a train to catch!"

"You ladies need a ride? I think I might be going your way," said Jack.

The three of them walked down the steps, waved goodbye to Mrs. Dorothy, and climbed into Jack's Datsun.

"Nice ride, Jack. Is it yours?"

"Mum's," he replied.

"We're not quite done with our little mess, you know. In some ways, it feels okay to just walk away. Eye for an eye," said Maggie.

"Poetic justice," Jack replied, smiling. "I know. Almost seems right, but it's not. Before we get going, I'll make one quick call, okay?"

"Sure," said Maggie.

Jack pulled his cell phone out of his pocket, hit redial, and started talking.

"Hey, Sam. Yeah, doing good. You?"

Jack nodded his head, then continued. "Got a little present for you. No rush. Maybe pick it up tomorrow? Yeah, it'll keep. I'll text you the address."

He looked at Maggie and smiled. She nodded.

"If it's your mess, you'd better clean it up," she could hear her dad say.

About the Author

Heather Glenn Vines, author of a number of children's books including *Love, Sun* and *That's One Odd Duck*, lives in Montana on Flathead Lake and in Portland, Oregon. A former advertising copywriter in New York City, she has a Master's degree in English Literature from Virginia Tech.

Explore Heather Glenn Vines' Children's Books
Little Books for Hearts & Minds

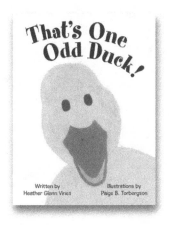

That's One Odd Duck

With big clumsy feet and a giant orange nose, Baxter isn't like any of his brothers and sisters. They run; he waddles. They meow; he quacks. Being different, though, turns out to be a very good thing for this little duck who discovers he isn't a kitten after all.

Love, Sun

When the sun sets and her job is done, who watches over all her little children? *Love, Sun* is a beautifully illustrated bedtime story from the sun's perspective. We follow her throughout her day up until nightfall, when she graciously steps aside and lets someone else take over.

For more information, visit:
VinesLines.com

CPSIA information can be obtained
at www.ICGtesting.com
Printed in the USA
LVHW102111020922
727390LV00002B/272